ZIMBABWE AFTER MUGABE

HEARING

BEFORE THE

SUBCOMMITTEE ON AFRICA, GLOBAL HEALTH, GLOBAL HUMAN RIGHTS, AND INTERNATIONAL ORGANIZATIONS

OF THE

COMMITTEE ON FOREIGN AFFAIRS
HOUSE OF REPRESENTATIVES

ONE HUNDRED FIFTEENTH CONGRESS

SECOND SESSION

FEBRUARY 28, 2018

Serial No. 115–114

Printed for the use of the Committee on Foreign Affairs

Available via the World Wide Web: http://www.foreignaffairs.house.gov/ or
http://www.gpo.gov/fdsys/

U.S. GOVERNMENT PUBLISHING OFFICE

28–825PDF   WASHINGTON : 2018

CONTENTS

Page

WITNESSES

LETTERS, STATEMENTS, ETC., SUBMITTED FOR THE HEARING

APPENDIX

ZIMBABWE AFTER MUGABE

WEDNESDAY, FEBRUARY 28, 2018

House of Representatives,
Subcommittee on Africa, Global Health,
Global Human Rights, and International Organizations,
Committee on Foreign Affairs,
Washington, DC.

The subcommittee met, pursuant to notice, at 2:01 p.m., in room 2172, Rayburn House Office Building, Hon. Christopher H. Smith (chairman of the subcommittee) presiding.

Mr. Smith. The hearing will come to order, and welcome to all of you.

Today's hearing has been a long time in the making. For some 37 years, since the birth of modern Zimbabwe, Robert Mugabe has dominated the political landscape of this resource-rich and promising country: First, as Prime Minister, then as President, and always as strongman.

It was a 37-year rule which sadly betrayed the post-colonial aspirations of freedom, one which was marked by misrule, mismanagement, and mistreatment of Mugabe's fellow citizens.

For many Zimbabweans, and for many years, envisioning a Zimbabwe without Mugabe was considered a fool's errand. Elections, some more flawed than others, had come and gone, opportunities for reform fallen by the wayside. And through it all, the domineering presence of one man haunted the dreams of his countrymen.

Then in a matter of weeks, culminating last November, the landscape changed. The once invincible ruler in October 2017 set into motion a series of events which left him not only ousted from the Zimbabwe African National Union-Patriotic Front, or ZANU-PF, but pushed off his Presidential perch.

The drama began in earnest when Mugabe sought to prop up his wife Grace's standing as his designated successor by ousting one of his two Vice Presidents, Emmerson Mnangagwa, presumably to elevate his wife to the position, while simultaneously moving against Mnangagwa's allies in the government and in ZANU-PF, promoting a younger generation allied with Grace.

Mnangagwa was part of an older faction of ZANU-PF, the generation that fought for liberation with roots and strong connections in the military. As Rhodesian Bush War veterans and political survivors, Mnangagwa and his comrades could draw upon a reservoir of experience and cunning. They would not be so easily pushed aside.

While Mugabe sought to tighten the reins of control in favor of his wife and her allies, the other Vice President and head of the Zimbabwe Defence Forces, Constantino Chiwenga, made a bold statement on November 13, and I quote, ". . . matters of protecting our revolution, the military will not hesitate to step in."

This was declared treasonous, but before Chiwenga himself could be arrested, the Zimbabwe Defence Forces did, in fact, step in and confine the long-serving President to his quarters, while taking control of key points around the country.

What followed were spontaneous popular demonstrations against Robert Mugabe, indicating that the spell had been broken. ZANU-PF convened a meeting which declared Mnangagwa to be interim leader of the party. And in the face of impeachment proceedings against Mugabe, the 93-year-old President reluctantly stepped down, allowing Mnangagwa to assume the vacancy.

This series of actions preserved the veneer of constitutional process such that neither our country nor the African Union could label the events that took place a coup. Indeed, if it were a coup, it was a popularly supported one and one which subsequently received high court ratification.

So where does that leave us? Who is Emmerson Mnangagwa, the man who was sworn in as Zimbabwe's President on November 21?

Critics have called him the "crocodile" and recall his role as Mugabe's right-hand man and confidante, including during the brutal period in the early 1980s, when in the newly independent nation, Mugabe waged an internal campaign of repression against fellow revolutionary leader Joshua Nkomo, killing thousands of ethnic minority individuals who were followers of Nkomo.

During this time, Mugabe was assisted by military advisers from East Germany and North Korea, and his Minister of State Security, one Emmerson Mnangagwa.

Others more charitably admit that Mnangagwa was, indeed, once the crocodile, but maintain that he has changed, undergoing a religious conversion to evangelical Christianity. Indeed, his rhetoric since acceding to power has been reassuring, stating that he will restore democracy, rule of law, economic prosperity, and trade, while addressing endemic corruption.

On the issue of land tenure, he said he would end the seizures of property that Mugabe had used to punish enemies and reward cronies.

So they stand at a crossroads, perhaps facing a once-in-a-lifetime opportunity where Zimbabwe can chart a new course. Yet, we cannot forget and cannot be Pollyanish about it, nor disregard the wise words of Pete Townshend, who once said: "Meet the new boss. Same as the old boss. We won't get fooled again." Hopefully, none of that will be true.

On the issue of land seizures, for example, one notes that the newly retired general, as of December 28, 2017, the new Vice President, Constantino Chiwenga, who issued the treasonous challenge that led to Mugabe's ouster, is alleged to be a beneficiary of Mugabe's past largesse with other people's land. This is perhaps something which all of our witnesses today might want to speak to and clarify.

Indeed, as we attempt to read the tea leaves and discern what is in the future, we will be assisted by a stellar panel. While the State Department is unable to send a witness due to the immediacy of issues concerning the budget and Secretary of State Tillerson's impending trip to Africa, we have with us a former Ambassador of the United States, a very distinguished one at that, to Zimbabwe, as well as one of the key implementers of our democracy promotion policy in Zimbabwe.

We also have two Zimbabweans with us who are extremely well-versed and involved in the contemporary events in the country.

Today's hearing will look at the prospects for true democratic and governance reform, as well as the potential restoration of the rule of law. We truly hope that the arrival of a new government signals an opportunity for establishing a mutually beneficial relationship between the United States and Zimbabwe, and as the near future unfolds, events will allow us to reevaluate some of the sanctions that were imposed during the Mugabe years.

I would like to yield to my good friend and ranking member, Ms. Bass.

Okay. I will go to the chairman of the full committee.

Mr. ROYCE. I thank you. Congresswoman, thanks for allowing me to make an opening statement as well. And let me thank the both of you for your engagement on the continent, an engagement that has been consistent. And now there are some new opportunities.

I recall just about 20 years ago that I was in Harare and Bulawayo, and the emotional feeling of listening to Morgan Tsvangirai's supporters, and later him, speak about that issue of human rights, and going back later and not being able to get into the country, but having the opportunity to meet with some of those who had been tortured or had gone through a lot. And not just members of that Movement for Democratic Change. Also some of the ZANU-PF members who I talked to who tried to speak out. Tried to speak out.

And this is the problem of a society in which you have a totalitarian aspect that takes hold. And slowly, economic freedom erodes, opportunity erodes, and you have a situation where people have absolutely no ability any longer to choose their leaders or to choose the future for their country.

Now that is in play again. Now there is that opportunity. And I know the international community and NGOs and those concerned with leading on human rights have great hope at this point in time.

We watched here on this committee as the regime stripped away the opportunity that existed for people. But Zimbabwe, as you all know, was once the breadbasket for the region. And we had a Zimbabwe Democracy and Economic Recovery Act that we passed here in 2001 in which we tried to shape events there.

But today we have got to be clearheaded, I think, as we look at the prospects for democracy. Some members of the current government did have a role in the oppressive and violent policies that characterized the Mugabe regime. Some are responsible for some of the worst abuses.

But on the other hand, we do have that opportunity. And we have a lot of people in Zimbabwe today who have second thoughts and are looking back at what happened and how it happened. And I think a lot of those individuals are really determined to make certain that Zimbabwe now has that chance to chart its future.

We remember Morgan Tsvangirai, recently deceased of course, but we remember him for his unwavering struggle. And I think the July elections that are quickly approaching, this will be an important test. I think the people of Zimbabwe, at this point, it is their time. It is their opportunity.

But elections have got to be credible. They have got to be peaceful. They must be transparent. I think the government must take steps to combat corruption, to protect freedom of expression, to end state-backed violence and intimidation, and address other issues in terms of the rights of the people.

The U.S. should see meaningful progress toward these reforms before we revise our current policy, because we need a little leverage in this. And I think the U.S. would be a partner in all of these reform efforts. I think we will have bipartisan support for that partnership. And I think it is through these reforms that we will see again prosperity and opportunity.

I am not sure I should say "see again." I think maybe see for the first time. Because Zimbabwe had a long, struggled, tortured history. But finally, that chapter is over. And like the previous chapters in that history, it has been tough on the people of Zimbabwe. So let's all of us do what we can do, but I appreciate these witnesses traveling so far to testify.

I have got a meeting with an Ambassador here adjacent. But I want to again thank you, Chris, Chairman, and thank you very much, Congresswoman, for your engagement here.

Mr. SMITH. Thank you very much, Chairman Royce. Thank you for taking the time from what I know is an extremely busy schedule to be here. Your commitment and concern about Africa is legendary. So thank you for being here.

I would like to now yield to Karen Bass again, the ranking member, for any opening comments she might have.

Ms. BASS. Thank you, Mr. Chair, and ditto to the words that you just said about our chairman and his long history of support for Africa.

In November 2017, we all know that Robert Mugabe's 30-year Presidency ended. The circumstances under which he left office included a military operation, paramilitary proceedings, preliminary proceedings to impeach him, and most importantly, ordinary citizens dancing, cheering, and waving flags in the streets.

Why would Zimbabweans march alongside the military celebrating and demanding the resignation of Mugabe? Well, there are a host of reasons. The answer is pretty simple. As our witness Dr. Dendere will point out, for the first time Zimbabweans felt a sense of hope. Hope for their political and economic future.

There are many ways to read this current moment, and today we will attempt to consider how the U.S. can best reengage the Government of Zimbabwe. It will be tempting to tie everything to the next elections, to focus on allowing international observers, ensuring free, fair, and transparent elections to make sure that elections take place this year. And although we know this is important, normalizing relations with Zimbabwe requires more than a good election.

First, we have to consider that while this is not exactly a traditional military coup, it also wasn't a regular democratic transition of power. The military has a long history of partisanship with the ruling party interfering in the nation's political electoral affairs in ways that adversely affected the ability of citizens to vote freely. The partisanship of the security forces' leadership has translated into abuses by these forces against civil society, activists, journalists, and members and supporters of the opposition political party the Movement for Democratic Change.

The military played a key role in this transition and while some citizens expressed support for the transition of power, recent polling by the Afrobarometer shows that 69 percent of Zimbabweans are against military rule and 75 percent prefer democracy over any other form of government. This should give the Mnangagwa government a sense of what their citizens want.

Going forward, it will be important for the military to show that they will comply with the Constitution by staying out of the electoral process. The military should have no role in the upcoming political campaigns.

And I don't say this lightly. Everyone in this room is well-aware that here in the U.S. we are going through our own challenges with protecting U.S. electoral systems, including dealing with external interference to voter suppression. It is vitally important that countries not leave their political systems vulnerable.

A key part of ensuring the credibility of Zimbabwe's elections is to ensure that the electoral commission is independent, impartial, and nonpartisan. It is also essential that every citizen has the right to voice their views and opinions individually and collectively; that they have the ability to vote; that elections are free from violence; that opposition parties are able to operate and campaign freely without harassment; that the election is transparent; that the institutions can operate independently; and that the military does not engage in politics.

The current administration has an opportunity to break with the past to set the country on a new course by strengthening democratic institutions and rule of law, improving human rights and civil liberties, including allowing freedom of assembly and expression, and enacting economic and political reforms that will better the lives of Zimbabwean citizens. But they also have an opportunity to address many of the challenges that were not resolved during Mugabe's Presidency so that the country can truly enter a post-Mugabe era.

Mr. SMITH. Thank you very much, Ms. Bass.

I would now like to welcome our very, very distinguished panel, beginning with Ambassador Charles Ray who served as U.S. Ambassador to Zimbabwe as well as Cambodia.

Ambassador Ray retired in 2012—although he can't call what he is doing now retirement. He is now more active than ever—after a 30-year career in the U.S. Foreign Service that included postings in China, Thailand, Sierra Leone, and Vietnam. He also served as the first U.S. Consul General in Ho Chi Minh City, Vietnam.

Prior to joining the Foreign Service, Ambassador Ray spent 20 years in the U.S. Army, retiring with the rank of major during his Army career. He did two tours in Vietnam, served in military intelligence, special operations, and public affairs, with assignments in Germany, Korea, Vietnam, Panama, and the United States.

Since his retirement, he has been a writer, lecturer, and consultant, and has done research on leadership and ethics. He is the author of more than 60 books of fiction and nonfiction.

Ambassador Ray is a member of the American Foreign Service Association. He is on the board of directors of the American Academy of Diplomacy and the Cold War Museum at Vint Hill, Virginia, and is director of communications for the Association of Black American Ambassadors.

We welcome your testimony, Mr. Ambassador, and thank you for your service to our country, both in uniform and in the Foreign Service.

We will then hear from Elizabeth Lewis, who is a regional deputy director for Africa at the International Republican Institute, or IRI, where she oversees field offices in 12 nations, including Zimbabwe. In her role at IRI she focuses on the implementation of local governance, elections, conflict mitigation, and civil society programs.

Since 2009 Ms. Lewis has managed IRI programs in sub-Saharan Africa, specializing in the Horn and Southern African regions. She observed Tunisia's December 2014 Presidential runoff election, Nigeria's March 2015 general election, and Ghana's December 2016 national elections.

Ms. Lewis has a BA in political science and economics from St. Mary's College in Maryland and an MS in political economy of late development from the London School of Economics and Political Science.

Thank you for being here as well.

We will then hear from Ben Freeth, MBE. He is the executive director of the Mike Campbell Foundation, an organization fighting for human rights and property rights in Zimbabwe.

Together, with his late father-in-law, Mike Campbell, the owner of Mount Carmel Farm in central Zimbabwe, Mr. Freeth took President Robert Mugabe's government to court in the Southern African Development Community's regional court, the SADC Tribunal, contesting the regime's ongoing attempts to unlawfully seize Mr. Campbell's farm and for engaging in racial discrimination and violence against White commercial farmers and their workers.

Mr. Campbell, his wife, and Mr. Freeth were abducted and tortured in 2008 and later suffered the destruction of their home by fire. Since 2011, Mr. Freeth has been involved in initiatives to restore the SADC Tribunal after it was shut down by the SADC head of state, thus denying individual citizens access to the human rights court.

Mr. Freeth also works closely with Foundations for Farming, an organization that provides training in conservation and agriculture and teaches impoverished farm workers and others how to feed their families.

We welcome back Mr. Freeth, who testified before this subcommittee in 2015.

Then we will hear from Dr. Chipo Dendere, who is a Zimbabwean political scientist currently serving as a Consortium for Faculty Diversity fellow and visiting assistant professor of political science at Amherst College.

Dr. Dendere's research expertise is in democracy, elections, and migration, with a regional interest in African politics. She writes about the impact of voter exit, migration, and remittances on the survival of authoritarian regimes. Her new research is on the role of technology and social media in new democracies.

We welcome her testimony before the subcommittee and thank her for being here as well.

Mr. Ambassador, the floor is yours.

STATEMENT OF THE HONORABLE CHARLES A. RAY (FORMER U.S. AMBASSADOR TO ZIMBABWE)

Ambassador RAY. Thank you, Mr. Chairman and Ms. Bass. I am very honored to be able to appear here today to discuss the path forward in U.S.-Zimbabwe relations.

I served as U.S. Ambassador to Zimbabwe from 2009 to 2012, during the period of the ZANU-PF/MDC coalition government, a time of relative peace and a certain amount of economic stability, but, unfortunately, also a time of lost opportunities to put Zimbabwe on the path of a truly representative government and a prosperous economy.

Most Americans probably know very little about Zimbabwe, but for a brief time this past November it was again very prominent in the American media. After several weeks of increasing political turmoil, primarily within Mugabe's ruling party, the First Vice President, Emmerson Mnangagwa, was accused of disloyalty and sacked. He then fled to South Africa, claiming that his life was in danger.

Around the same time, Mugabe's wife Grace began to appear more and more in public, stating that she should be the one to succeed the aging leader, statements that Mugabe, to his discredit, did nothing to deny.

In an unprecedented for Zimbabwe move, General Constantine Chiwenga, chief of the defence staff, made a public statement that the military would not stand idly by and allow liberation figures to be removed from the government or from the party.

He was accused of treason. But shortly thereafter, the military made its move. It took control of key installations in Harare, placed Mugabe and his family under effective house arrest—although it was very quick to publicly state this is not a coup. But as one opposition figure said, if it looks like a duck and it walks like a duck, it is a duck.

Make no mistake about it, even though it was a palace coup with the military moving against members of its own party or the party that it supports, it was, in fact, a coup d'etat, a relatively nonviolent one and done in a most unusual way.

Mugabe was allowed to meet with the press, to engage in a phone conversation with the former President of South Africa, and his meeting with the leader of the coup, with General Chiwenga, at least on the surface, appeared to be very cordial, and he was even allowed to call a cabinet meeting. But it was still a change of government initiated by force of arms, rather than through the ballot box.

However, how the military's actions in this case will be dealt with I think is something for Zimbabweans to handle. For the rest of the world, and for the U.S. in particular, I think the key questions now are: Where is Zimbabwe going from here, and what role should we play in that journey?

We should start, I think, with a bit of background on the new interim President, Emmerson Mnangagwa. I think the question on many minds is: Will he be any different from Mugabe?

He is, after all, someone who worked closely with Mugabe for more than 37 years after the country's independence and served as an intelligence officer during the war for independence, and who, because of his actions in support of the crackdown on the Ndebele political opposition in the 1980s and MDC supporters in the 1990s, has earned the nickname "the crocodile."

Prior to being appointed to the First Vice President position, Mnangagwa served as Defence Minister and also as Justice Minister. Though he lacks Mugabe's charisma, it appears that he enjoys the firm support of many of the senior military officials.

I think, moving forward, his first priority will be to reassert control over ZANU-PF, a party that is fractured along generational lines with many of those in their forties and fifties, known as the G-40, supporting Grace Mugabe against the older liberation era party members.

A united ZANU-PF is essential if the party is to retain power. This won't be an easy task for Mnangagwa as the rift between the two demographics was worsened by some of the actions and rhetoric during September-November of last year.

The issue is further complicated by the presence of former ZANU-PF number two Joice Mujuru. She was First Vice President until she was canned a few years ago. She is now the head of the People First or ZIM-PF Party.

Until Grace Mugabe engineered her ouster, she was in competition with Mnangagwa to be Mugabe's successor. A veteran of the liberation struggle, as a fighter with a fierce reputation, she also enjoys some military support, although probably not as much as Mnangagwa.

The second priority, I believe, will be to ensure ZANU-PF's continued control of power in the country. If he can somehow pull all of the factions together and overcome the possible threat from Mujuru, he will have to decide whether or not to proceed with elections in July 2018. I realize that he has publicly stated that he will, but we will have to see what really happens.

While violence and chicanery are still possibilities that cannot be cavalierly dismissed, a united ZANU-PF is likely to be able to do well against the current opposition party lineup. The Movement for Democratic Change, or MDC, is still split between the faction led by the late Morgan Tsvangirai, now with an interim President, Nelson Chamisa, and the one led by Welshman Ncube.

As the parties that pose the greatest challenge to ZANU-PF, especially in the urban areas, if they were united, they would surely do well, but it is unlikely that they will unite. The remainder of the opposition parties, with the exception of Joice Mujuru's party, will only take votes away from the two MDCs, which is to ZANU-PF's advantage, unfortunately.

In the rural areas, ZANU-PF has, in the past at least, had an advantage and Mnangagwa is sure to capitalize on this. So while it is too early to predict that the 2018 elections will be free, fair, and nonviolent, let's assume for a moment that they will be. Where do we go from that point?

During my time as Ambassador to Zimbabwe, one of the most frequent topics of conversation was U.S. sanctions. Put in place in response to the violent land seizures and electoral violence of the late 1990s, the Zimbabwe Democracy and Economic Recovery Act, or ZDERA, was passed in December 2001, and a Presidential executive order targeting individuals and entities involved in the violence and other anti-democratic acts was issued in March 2003.

Both of these actions were intended to encourage a return to democracy and representative government, something that had not happened by the time of my arrival in 2009. After the MDC won the 2008 elections, although without the necessary 51 percent majority, there was more violence. But under South African pressure, a coalition government was formed.

That government, with the MDC in a decidedly subordinate position to ZANU-PF, lasted until the 2014 elections in which ZANU-PF got the required majority and subsequently formed a government without the MDC.

The sanctions, in my view, were clearly not having the desired effect, and Mugabe's party's hardliners were using their existence as an excuse for every ill that the country suffered. My response to the many questions of, "When will the sanctions be lifted?" was, "When there is a return to nonviolent elections and democracy."

In fact, during one of my final media interviews before I departed in 2012, I said that sanctions were a response to a violent electoral process. A credible electoral process free of violence would make our current policy somewhat irrelevant.

If this year's elections are held, if they are determined to be credible, and if there is no violence, the ball will be in our court. If we truly want to see Zimbabwe develop to its potential, we must be prepared to work with the winner of a credible, nonviolent election regardless of the political party.

Even if the election is credible and nonviolent, any new government is almost certain to contain officials who bring a lot of historical baggage with them to their positions. I firmly believe, however, that we should in such a situation put the past behind us and focus on the policy statement in the introduction of ZDERA: "It is the policy of the United States to support the people of Zimbabwe in their struggle to effect peaceful, democratic change, achieve broad-based and equitable economic growth, and restore the rule of law." I leave development of the precise modalities of our actions to the policymakers and the professionals in the foreign and civil services of our foreign affairs agencies, primarily State and AID, but I would offer a few humble suggestions on a way forward.

First, I think we should instruct our Embassy in Harare to make contact with Mnangagwa and his current government to reiterate firmly our policy regarding sanctions and to inform him that if upcoming elections are credible and nonviolent we are prepared to recognize and work with the new government.

While we would continue to monitor the human rights situation, our initial focus should be on actions to reinvigorate the country's economy and empower the private sector to revitalize the agricultural sector, and rebuild stagnant industries with a view to creating meaningful employment and broad economic security.

We should encourage the new government to develop an investor-friendly climate, take steps to curb corruption, while at the same time encourage American businesses to explore the opportunities to increase two-way trade and investment.

You might note, I said nothing about lifting sanctions. I think that that should be the stick. The carrot, I think, would be our offer to deal with the government. The stick is, if they don't deal, sanctions stay in place.

During my time as Ambassador, we experimented with a local economic development program modeled on an Asian village financing scheme that I encountered when I lived in Korea back in the 1970s. Women in a few poor rural villages were taught to organize local savings clubs in which deposits were loaned out to members at low interest for income-producing ventures. These programs, though they were known to the government, were outside government control, and within months of establishment, totally self-reliant.

Consideration should be given to implementing such a program in rural and suburban communities throughout the country. People who are economically self-sufficient are less vulnerable to political exploitation.

The elephant in the room which can't be ignored is the Zimbabwean military. Existing laws and regulation will limit what we can do with the military. But for the long-term, peaceful development of Zimbabwe, at some point we will have to figure out a way to work with this institution.

Initially, I believe the primary focus should be on inculcating in the military establishment an ethos of service to the nation as a whole rather than identification with a specific political party.

In my limited contact with senior military officials when I was Ambassador, I was convinced that there exists within the military establishment a small cadre of people who would like to be professional and who would like to depoliticize the institution. The challenge will be to identify those individuals and develop effective ways of working with them.

One possibility, I think, might be to establish a working relationship with the SADC peacekeeping academy, which happens to be located in Harare, and allowing properly vetted Zimbabwean military officials to participate in courses of instruction on military professionalism.

Again, I leave it to State and Defense, working with Congress, to determine if such a program could be implemented and just how it should.

While I have in making these recommendations assumed that elections will be held in July 2018 and assumed that they will be credible and nonviolent, I must make clear at this point that I am not making a prediction. I do believe that if everyone in Zimbabwe approaches the coming months with an earnest desire to see the country pull itself out of the doldrums and take its rightful place in the region and in the world, it can happen.

If it does happen, if everyone then puts the past behind them and focuses on the future, a new and more vibrant Zimbabwe can arise phoenix-like from the ashes.

Thank you.

[The prepared statement of Ambassador Ray follows:]

Statement by Ambassador (ret) Charles Ray

To the Africa Subcommittee of the

House Foreign Affairs Committee

THE FUTURE OF ZIMBABWE AFTER MUGABE

Chairman and distinguished members of the subcommittee, I am honored to be able to appear before you today to discuss the path forward in US-Zimbabwe relations. I served as U.S. Ambassador to Zimbabwe from 2009 to 2012, during the period of the ZANU-PF/MDC coalition government, a time of relative peace and economic stability, but, unfortunately, also a time of lost opportunities to put Zimbabwe on the path of truly representative government and a prosperous economy.

Most American today know very little about Zimbabwe, but for a brief time in November 2017, it was again prominent in the American mass media.

After several weeks of increasing political turmoil, primarily within Mugabe's ruling ZANU-PF party, the first vice president, Emmerson D. Mnangagwa was accused of disloyalty and sacked. He then fled to South Africa, claiming that his life was in danger. Around this same time, Mugabe's wife, Grace, began to appear more and more in public, making statements that she should be the one to succeed the aging leader, pronouncements that Mugabe did nothing to deny. In an unprecedented—for Zimbabwe—move, Constantine Chiwenga, chief of the Zimbabwe Defense Staff, made a public statement that the military would not stand idly by and allow liberation figures to be removed from government or the party.

Shortly thereafter the military made its move. It took control of key installations in Harare, and placed Mugabe and his family under effective house arrest—although, it was quick to publicly announce that what it was doing was not a coup. As one opposition figure said, though, if it walks like a duck and quacks like a duck, it's a duck. It was a palace coup, with the army moving against elements of its own party, but make no mistake about it, it was a coup d'état. Relatively nonviolent, and done in a most unusual way; Mugabe was allowed to meet the press, to phone the South African president, to meet with the coup leader in what on the surface appeared a cordial encounter, and even to call a cabinet meeting; it was still a change of government initiated by force of arms rather than the ballot box.

How the military's actions will be dealt with is something for Zimbabweans to decide. For the rest of the world, and the United States in particular, the key questions are; where does Zimbabwe go from here, and what role should we play in that journey?

We should start with a bit of background on Zimbabwe's new ruler, Emmerson Mnangagwa. The question on many minds is, will he be any different from Mugabe? He is, after all, someone who worked closely with Mugabe for more than 37 years after the country's independence, who served as an intelligence officer during the war for independence, and who, because of his actions in support the crackdown on Ndebele political opposition in the 1980s, and MDC supporters in the 1990s, has earned the nickname, 'Crocodile.' Prior to being appointed to the first vice president position, Mnangagwa served as defense minister and justice minister. Though he lacks Mugabe's charisma, he enjoys the support of most senior military officials.

Moving forward, his first priority will be to reassert control over ZANU-PF, a party that has fractured along generational lines, with many of those in their 40s and 50s, known as the G-40, supporting Grace Mugabe against the older liberation-era party members. A united ZANU-PF is essential if the party is to retain power. This won't be an easy task for Mnangagwa, as the rift between the two demographics was worsened by some of the actions and rhetoric during September-November of last year. The issue is further complicated by the presence of former ZANU-PF number two, Joice Mujuru's Zimbabwe People First (ZIM-PF) Party. Mujuru, until Grace Mugabe engineered her ouster, was first vice president, and at the time was in competition with Mnangagwa, a successor to Mugabe. A veteran of the liberation struggle, as a fighter with a fierce reputation, she also enjoys some military support, although probably not as much as Mnangagwa.

Mnangagwa's second priority, I believe, will be to ensure ZANU-PF's continued control of the reins of power in the country. If he can somehow pull all the ZANU factions together, and overcome the possible threat from Mujuru, he will have to decide whether or not to proceed with elections in July 2018. He has indicated that he will do so. While violence and chicanery are still possibilities that can't be cavalierly dismissed, a united ZANU-PF is likely to be able to do well against the current opposition party lineup. The Movement for Democratic Change (MDC) is still split between the faction led by Morgan Tsvangirai and the one led by Welshman Ncube. As the parties that pose the greatest challenge to ZANU-PF in the urban areas, if they were united, they might do well, but it is unlikely that they will merge. The remainder of the opposition parties, with the exception of ZIM-PF, will only take votes away from MDC, which is to ZANU-PF's advantage. In the rural areas, ZANU-PF has, in the past at least, had an advantage, and Mnangagwa is sure to capitalize on this.

So, while it's too early to predict that the 2018 elections will be free, fair and nonviolent, let us assume, for the moment that they will be.

Where do *we* go from that point?

During my time as US Ambassador to Zimbabwe, one of the most frequent topics of conversation was US sanctions. Put in place in response to the violent land seizures and electoral violence of the late 1990s, the Zimbabwe Democracy and Economic Recovery Act was enacted in December 2001, and a presidential executive order, targeting individuals and entities involved in the violence and antidemocratic acts was issued in March 2003. Both actions were intended to encourage a return to democracy, something that had not happened by the time of my arrival in 2009. After the MDC won the 2008 elections, although without the necessary 51% majority, there was more violence, but under South African pressure, a coalition government was formed. That government, with the MDC in a subordinate position to ZANU-PF, lasted until the 2014 elections, in which ZANU-PF got the required majority and subsequently formed a government without MDC.

The sanctions, in my view, were clearly not having the desired effect, and Mugabe's party hardliners were using their existence as an excuse for all of the country's ills.

My response to the many queries of, 'when will sanctions be lifted/', was, 'when there is a return to nonviolent elections and democracy. In fact, during one of my final media interviews before my departure in 2012, at the end of my tour, I said, "Sanctions were a response to a violent electoral process. A credible electoral process, free of violence, would make our current policies irrelevant."

If this year's elections are head, they are determined to be credible, and there is no violence, the ball will be in our court.

If we truly want to see Zimbabwe develop to its potential, we must be prepared to work with the winner of a credible, nonviolent election, regardless of the political party. Even if the election is credible and nonviolent, any new government is almost certain to contain officials who bring a lot of historical baggage with them to the positions they occupy. I firmly believe, however, that we should, in such a situation, put the past behind us and focus on the policy statement in the introduction of the Zimbabwe Democracy and Economic Recovery Act of 2001; 'it is the policy of the United States to support the people of Zimbabwe in their struggle to effect peaceful, democratic change, achieve broad-based and equitable economic growth, and restore the rule of law."

I leave development of the precise modalities of our actions to the policy makers and the professionals in the Foreign and Civil services of our foreign affairs agencies, primarily State and USAID, but I would offer a few suggestions on the way forward.

First, we should instruct our embassy in Harare to establish contact with Mnangagwa and his current government to reiterate our policy regarding sanctions, and to inform him that, if upcoming elections are credible and nonviolent, we are prepared to recognize and work with the new government. While we should continue to monitor the human rights situation, our initial focus should be on actions to reinvigorate the country's economy and empower the private sector to revitalize the agricultural sector, and rebuild stagnant industries, with a view to creating meaningful employment and broad economic security. We should encourage the new government to develop an investor-friendly climate, and take steps to curb corruption, while at the same time, encouraging American business to explore opportunities to increase two-way trade and investment.

During my time as ambassador, we experimented with a local economic development program modeled on an Asian village financing scheme. Women in a few poor rural villages were taught to organize local savings clubs, in which deposits were loaned out to members at low interest rates for income-producing ventures. These programs, though known to the government, were outside government control, and within months of establishment, totally self-reliant. Consideration should be given to implementing such a program in rural and suburban communities country-wide. People who are economically self-sufficient are less vulnerable to political exploitation.

The elephant in the room, which can't be entirely ignored, is the Zimbabwean military. Existing laws and regulations will limit what we can do with the military, but for the long term, peaceful development of Zimbabwe, at some point we will have to figure out a way to work with this institution. Initially, I believe the primary focus should be on inculcating in the military establishment an ethos of service to the nation as a whole rather than identification with a specific political party. In my limited contact with senior military officials when I was ambassador, I was convinced that there exists within the military establishment a cadre of people who would like to professionalize and depoliticize the institution. The challenge will be to identify those individuals, and develop effective ways of working with them. One possibility might be to establish a working relationship with the SADC Peacekeeping Academy, which is located in Harare, and allowing Zimbabwean military participation in courses of instruction on military professionalism. I leave it to State and Defense, working with the congress, to determine just how such a program would be implemented.

While I have, in making these recommendations, assumed that elections will be held in July 2018, and that they will be credible and nonviolent, I must make clear at this point that I am not making a prediction. I do believe that if everyone approaches the coming months with an earnest desire to see Zimbabwe pull itself out of the doldrums and take its rightful place in the region and the world, it *can* happen. If it *does* happen, if everyone then puts the past behind them and focuses on the future, a new and more vibrant Zimbabwe can arise Phoenix-like from the ashes.

Mr. SMITH. Thank you so very much, Ambassador Ray.
Ms. Lewis.

STATEMENT OF MS. ELIZABETH LEWIS, REGIONAL DEPUTY DIRECTOR, AFRICA DIVISION, INTERNATIONAL REPUBLICAN INSTITUTE

Ms. LEWIS. Chairman Smith and Ranking Member Bass, it is an honor to testify before you today on the upcoming elections in Zimbabwe and the prospects for genuine democratic reform following the end of President Mugabe's 37-year rule.

I work for the International Republican Institute, which is a nonpartisan, nonprofit organization that is committed to advancing freedom and democracy worldwide. Since the early 1990s, IRI has supported pro-democracy activists in their struggle to bring real and lasting democratic reform to Zimbabwe.

Over the course of the last few months, Zimbabwe has turned a page in its history. On the evening of November 14, several leaders within the Zimbabwe Defence Forces led a coup against the government of President Robert Mugabe, which ended in his resignation a few days later. Then, just 2 weeks ago today, opposition leader and former Prime Minister Morgan Tsvangirai succumbed to his battle with cancer.

The departure of both Mugabe and Tsvangirai has upset the political order, and while some see the present situation as an opportunity for positive change, it is also a very fragile period for the country.

ZANU-PF remains in full control of Zimbabwe's governing institutions and chose former Vice President Emmerson Mnangagwa to serve as the country's third President. Mnangagwa's reputation precedes him, leaving many, including myself, skeptical of the prospects for genuine democratic reform under his leadership. One of his first acts as President, for instance, was to appoint a 22-member cabinet that included ZANU-PF hardliners and several military leaders who led the coup to put him in power.

Meanwhile, Zimbabwe's fractured political opposition is represented by several loose and evolving coalitions of political parties from both the historical opposition, including Tsvangirai's MDC-T, and defectors from ZANU-PF, including Joice Mujuru.

To date, the three main opposition coalitions, which include the MDC Alliance, the People's Rainbow Coalition, and CODE, have been unable to unite under a single cohesive electoral and governing coalition.

According to Zimbabwe's 2013 Constitution, barring a dissolution of Parliament, the 2018 elections must occur between July 23 and August 22. In recent statements, though, President Mnangagwa indicated the elections would occur before July and that they would be free, fair, credible, and free of violence.

However, in observing the biometric voter registration process that began on September 14, the Zimbabwe Election Support Network, or ZESN, indicated that turnout for the registration process was low, particularly among young people. The group cited limited voter education, intimidation of registrants, and misrepresentation of ID requirements as contributing factors to low turnout.

The challenge of high rates of voter illiteracy must be addressed through extensive voter education efforts in the leadup to election day. However, the short and still unannounced electoral timeline, combined with the challenges of misinformation, fears of violence, and the historical legacy of election fraud, makes all of this a significant undertaking.

Additionally, the environment in which campaigns and elections occur must be conducive to genuine political competition. For this to happen, several laws in Zimbabwe used to limit freedom of speech, freedom of assembly, and freedom of the press, and also restrict access to information, must be repealed or reformed to align with the 2013 Constitution.

Finally, the importance of a viable opposition capable of competing in the electoral process cannot be understated. A critical benchmark for the opposition in the coming elections is the prevention of a supermajority in the National Assembly, to prevent, among other things, amendments to the Constitution that would restrict political space and fundamental freedoms or grant additional powers to the Presidency.

It is vital that the U.S. stand by the Zimbabwean people in the movement for democratic reform in this period of transition, and with that goal in mind, I would like to offer the following recommendations.

First, the United States must be ardent in its support for free and fair elections. The citizen movements of last year are evidence of the strong desire for genuine change. The current government lacks electoral legitimacy and has a stated interest in returning to a full constitutional order.

Considering this alignment of interests, the U.S. must redouble its efforts to work with our Zimbabwean and regional partners, namely, SADC and the African Union, to stand for nothing less than a transition to democratic rule.

Relatedly, and over the longer term, the U.S. and our democratic allies must provide support to foster a competitive multiparty political system and the establishment of democratic institutions in Zimbabwe. This would include judicial, criminal justice, and security reform, opening the information space, the full implementation of the 2013 Constitution, responsive and participatory governance and service delivery, and a legitimate truth and reconciliation process.

Third, the United States should be prepared for numerous scenarios in a post-Mugabe era. ZANU-PF and the military complex that plays an increasingly visible role in the political party have everything to lose from a shift in the power dynamics of the country. Political repression and disregard for fundamental human and political rights is an ongoing problem in Zimbabwe and we need to be vigilant under the new dispensation in the leadup to and following elections.

And finally, the United States must hold the line with targeted sanctions and within international financial institutions. This is our strongest point of leverage in the push for democratic reform and respect for fundamental human rights and freedoms. Reforms must be required as a precondition for lending and debt or sanctions relief.

I thank you for your time and I look forward to your questions.
[The prepared statement of Ms. Lewis follows:]

Congressional Testimony

Zimbabwe After Mugabe

Testimony by Elizabeth Lewis
Regional Deputy Director, Africa Division
International Republican Institute

U.S. House Committee on Foreign Affairs
Subcommittee on Africa, Global Health, Global
Human Rights, and International Organizations

February 28, 2018

Introduction

Chairman Smith, Ranking Member Bass, and Members of the House Committee on Foreign Affairs, Subcommittee on Africa, Global Health, Global Human Rights, and International Organizations, it is an honor to testify before you today on the upcoming elections in Zimbabwe and the prospects for genuine democratic reform following the end of Robert Mugabe's 37-year rule.

The International Republican Institute (IRI) is a nonprofit, nonpartisan organization established in 1983 that is committed to advancing freedom and democracy worldwide. Since the early 1990s, IRI has supported pro-democracy activists in their struggle to bring real and lasting democratic reform to Zimbabwe, with activities including capacity-building support for democratic political parties, public opinion research, civic education, and fostering citizen and civil society engagement with local elected officials to address service delivery challenges.

Over the course of the last four months, Zimbabwe has turned a page in its political history. On the evening of 14 November 2017, several leaders within the Zimbabwe Defence Forces (ZDF) led a coup d'état against the government of Robert Mugabe, which led to Mugabe grudgingly resigning the presidency. Just two weeks ago today, the Zimbabwean opposition leader and former Prime Minister Morgan Tsvangirai succumbed to his battle with cancer – a significant loss to Zimbabweans' struggle for greater democracy in their country.

Zimbabwe has arrived at a critical waypoint in its journey toward democracy. The departure of Mugabe and Tsvangirai has upset the political order and left a leadership vacuum. Mugabe's ZANU-PF and Tsvangirai's Movement for Democratic Change (MDC-T) had already been engaged in succession battles prior to Mugabe's resignation and Tsvangirai's passing, and while some see the present situation as an opportunity for positive change, it is also a very fragile time for both the opposition and ruling factions. The next 6-12 months will prove decisive in determining the trajectory of Zimbabwe's democratic development.

Prospects for Democratic Reform: The Post-Coup Political Scene

Between the start of the military coup on November 14, 2017 and Mugabe's resignation on November 21, thousands of Zimbabweans poured onto the streets of Harare in a euphoric expression of free speech, shouting "Mugabe must go." This experience encouraged reformers and democracy activists to push for more significant change in the post-Mugabe period. While Mugabe's ouster was an important moment, it is important not to overstate its impact in achieving democratic change. At the same time Zimbabweans were on the streets clamoring for democratic change, the leaders of the coup were busy negotiating with ZANU-PF on plans for a tightly controlled non-democratic transition.

Today, ZANU-PF remains in full control of Zimbabwe's governing institutions and has chosen Mugabe's former vice president Emmerson Mnangagwa, who Mugabe fired in the days prior to his resignation, to serve as Zimbabwe's third president. In many ways, the country's leadership has engaged in an exercise of simply shifting the deck chairs. Mnangagwa, known from his days in the liberation struggle as the "Crocodile," was also Mugabe's Minister of Defence and Minister of Justice. While in charge of the country's security and intelligence apparatus, he is widely believed to have played a central role in *Gukurahundi* – a series of massacres of Ndebele citizens by the Zimbabwe National Army from 1983 to 1987.

Mnangagwa's reputation precedes him, leaving many skeptical of the prospect for genuine democratic reform under his leadership. In fact, one of his first acts as president represented just how little has changed since Mugabe's resignation. He appointed a new 22-member cabinet that included ZANU-PF hardliners with strong links to the liberation struggle and several military leaders who led the coup that put Mnangagwa into power. For instance, General Major Sibusiso Moyo, the soldier who announced Mugabe's ouster on the state broadcaster – now occupies a crucial cabinet post as Minister of Foreign Affairs.

Zimbabwe's fractured political opposition is represented by several loose and evolving coalitions of political parties from both the historical opposition – including Tsvangirai's MDC-T – and defectors from ZANU-PF, including Joice Mujuru and her National People's Party. To date, the three main opposition coalitions – the MDC Alliance, People's Rainbow Coalition, and Coalition of Democrats (CODE) – have been unable to unite under a single cohesive electoral and governing coalition. In fact, attempts to do so have only bred further disagreement over coalition leadership, member parties, and the division of elective seats.

Opposition parties have been in a state of general disarray since the 2013 elections. The days immediately surrounding Tsvangirai's death have put a spotlight on MDC-T's internal challenges to unify and compete for votes in just a few short months. While Tsvangirai's funeral reinvigorated many opposition supporters—bringing out thousands dressed in MDC-T's signature red color—violence and harassment targeting Vice President Thokozani Khupe, Secretary General Douglas Mwonzora and other senior party leaders cast a shadow over the occasion. This violence was fueled in part by a very public scramble for control of MDC-T following Tsvangirai's death.

Zimbabwe's Electoral Outlook

According to Zimbabwe's 2013 Constitution, barring a dissolution of Parliament, the 2018 elections must occur between July 23 and August 22. However, in recent statements (including at the World Economic Forum in Davos, Switzerland) President Mnangagwa indicated that elections would occur before July 2018, and pledged that "this time around, Zimbabwe is open and transparent. We want to have free, fair, credible elections, free of violence." Yet Zimbabwe's electoral history makes the prospect of holding free and fair elections in just a matter of months questionable; moreover, the Zimbabwe Electoral Commission (ZEC) has yet to announce its final operational plan for managing the elections.

The biometric voter registration (BVR) process began in Zimbabwe on September 14, 2017. In observing the process, the Zimbabwe Election Support Network (ZESN) indicated that turnout for the BVR process was low, particularly among young people. The group cited limited voter education, intimidation of registrants and misrepresentation of ID requirements (particularly in rural areas), and absence of signage marking registration centers as contributing factors. By the end of the voter registration blitz on December 19, the total number of voters registered amounted to only 65 percent of the ZEC's stated goal of 7.2 million.

Following calls by political and civil society stakeholders to extend the process arguing the coup changed people's motivations to vote, the ZEC held a "mop-up" exercise from January 10 to February 8, registering nearly 400,000 additional voters. However, ZESN reported that "it is clear that judging by the turnout in urban areas, there is still a large number of people that were not served by 08 February 2018, when the mop-up exercise ended." While voter registration continues until 12 days following the confirmation of candidates, the process now turns to the de-duplication procedure and inspection of the voter roll—important tasks that will need to be completed very quickly for elections to occur on time.

The challenge of high rates of voter illiteracy, as evidenced through the voter registration process, must be addressed through extensive voter education efforts in the lead up to Election Day. However, the short and still unannounced timeline to Election Day, combined with the challenges of misinformation, fears of violence and intimidation, and a historical legacy of election fraud— makes this a significant undertaking. The lack of transparency around many of the processes and decisions made by the ZEC and doubts over the competitiveness of the electoral environment will continue to feed high levels of voter apathy and political tension, especially among youth.

In addition to the technical capacity and financial needs required for the ZEC to hold a free, fair and credible election (which the African Union has pledged to support), the environment in which campaigns and elections occur must be conducive to genuine political competition. For this to happen, several laws in Zimbabwe used to limit freedom of speech, free press and assembly, and restrict access to information must be repealed or reformed to align with the 2013 Constitution. These repressive laws include the Public Order and Security Act, the Access to Information and Protection of Privacy Act, the Interception of Communications Act, and the Criminal Law (Codification and Reform) Act. The Electoral Law itself requires a substantial overhaul to align with the 2013 Constitution, including making the ZEC entirely independent and addressing the issue of diaspora voting.

Finally, the importance of a viable opposition capable of competing in the electoral process cannot be understated. A critical benchmark in achieving this is the prevention of a supermajority in the Zimbabwean National Assembly – which ZANU-PF currently has – to prevent further amendments to the 2013 Constitution that would restrict political space and fundamental freedoms or grant additional powers to the presidency. In the post-election period, it is critical that the opposition demonstrate its cohesiveness and capacity to serve as a check on government power and advocate for the interests and priorities of its constituents.

Recommendations

It is vital that the U.S. stand by the Zimbabwean people and the movement for democratic reform in this period of transition. With this goal in mind, I would like to offer the following recommendations:

The United States must be ardent in its support of free and fair elections. The citizen movements of last year, including #ThisFlag and Tajamuka, and the outpouring of citizens who took to the streets to celebrate the resignation of Mugabe are evidence of the strong desire for genuine change, and the 2018 elections will be a pivotal point for Zimbabwe. The current government lacks electoral legitimacy and has a stated interest in returning to full constitutional order. Considering this alignment of interests, the U.S. must offer its unwavering support for a free, fair, transparent and credible electoral process. Key U.S.-based, regional and international partners, including IRI, are already doing important work to support stakeholders including the ZEC, civil society and political parties ahead of the 2018 election, but this support must be expanded.

Key areas requiring additional attention include: civic education, in order to ensure that citizens are informed of the process and their rights ahead of Election Day; initiatives to combat fake news, disinformation and restrictions to the media and access to information; efforts to safeguard the vote, including the unhindered observation of the process by political parties and domestic and international observers; and activities to deliver an open and non-violent electoral process at all stages, from campaigning to electoral dispute resolution.

To achieve these objectives, the United States must redouble its efforts to work with our Zimbabwean and regional partners – especially the Southern African Development Community (SADC) and African Union – to stand for nothing less than a transition to democratic rule through a free, fair, transparent and credible electoral process.

Over the longer term, the U.S. and our democratic allies must provide support to foster a competitive multi-party-political system and the establishment of democratic institutions. As those of us who work in the field of democracy and governance assistance understand all-too-well, elections are just one part of a much larger democratic process. The overall health and maturation of Zimbabwe's democratic system requires a strong multi-party system.

Despite many challenges, Zimbabwe's democratic opposition has a number of advantages that should be recognized and leveraged, including a base of support among the population; access to young leaders rising through the ranks and taking on leadership roles; and governing experience under the Government of National Unity (a power-sharing agreement with ZANU-PF following the disputed 2008 elections), when despite the limitations of their position, they were able to achieve some successes in the management of the economy. A viable opposition is essential to a healthy Zimbabwean democracy, particularly in serving as a counterbalance to the ruling party's ability to expand its powers through the legislative process.

In addition to increasing political competition, other critical areas requiring attention include judicial, criminal justice and security reform; opening the information space; the full implementation of the 2013 Constitution; the need for responsive and participatory governance and service delivery; and a legitimate truth and reconciliation process. Again, engagement and support to Zimbabwean and regional partners in these areas is critical.

The United States should be prepared for numerous scenarios in a post-Mugabe era. The coming elections will be pivotal in determining the tolerance and space for future democratic development, but democratic progress is by no means certain. ZANU-PF and the military complex that plays an increasingly visible role in the party has everything to lose from a shift in the power dynamics of the country. Political repression and disregard for fundamental human and political rights is an ongoing problem in Zimbabwe, and we need to be vigilant under the new dispensation in the lead up to and following elections. U.S. policy toward Zimbabwe should be formulated to consider the multitude of scenarios that could unfold in the coming months.

The United States must hold the line with targeted sanctions and within international finance institutions to require the implementation of key reforms as a precursor to lending or debt/sanctions relief. Prior to the coup, one of the top issues discussed in the international arena regarding Zimbabwe was the clearing of its arrears with international finance institutions, namely the World Bank and African Development Bank, with the intent of making Zimbabwe eligible to participate in new lending programs. Under the new dispensation, debate over these issues has intensified, as the revival of Zimbabwe's long-suffering economy is a top priority for the Mnangagwa administration and the international community.

Other international partners, especially the United Kingdom, have been quick to support and engage with the new regime, and China has a historical legacy as a patron of ZANU-PF. Unlike the EU, which lifted sanctions on Zimbabwe on January 25 (except for two individuals: Robert and Grace Mugabe), the U.S. recently renewed its targeted sanctions on individuals including President Mnangagwa.

Sanctions and U.S. influence in international financial institutions are our strongest points of leverage in discussions over democratic reforms and respect for fundamental human rights and freedoms. The International Monetary Fund (IMF) announced on February 2 that it will only lend to Zimbabwe if it clears its debts with other multilateral institutions. Given the leadership role that the U.S. holds in the World Bank, it is vital that we hold the line until true progress and good will is demonstrated by the Mnangagwa administration and ZANU-PF officials.

I thank you for your time and look forward to your questions.

Mr. SMITH. Ms. Lewis, thank you very much for your recommendations and your testimony and your work. Thank you.

Mr. Freeth.

STATEMENT OF MR. BEN FREETH, EXECUTIVE DIRECTOR, MIKE CAMPBELL FOUNDATION

Mr. FREETH. Thank you very much. It is a great honor to be here once again in Washington, DC, and to be able to testify straight out of Zimbabwe as to where we are at this point. And it is really heartening to hear so much talk about the rule of law and the importance of the rule of law in our country.

And I think when we look back and we see what has taken place, with 25 percent of the population having left our country, with the education systems, which were the best in Africa, being trashed, with the social systems ending up in a total state of disrepair, with the economy in total tatters, with people queuing outside the banks just to try and withdraw their money, we have to look at the cause of these things. And the cause is the destruction of the rule of law and the destruction of property rights.

So we have just had a coup. We are 100 days in, or thereabouts, not quite. And where are we now? Are things getting better? Are reforms taking place? And I think if we listen to the rhetoric, it sounds all very good. There is a massive charm offensive taking place at the moment and many people are taken in by that charm offensive of the President and others in trying to make it look as though things have changed because the guy at the top has changed.

But when you look at it on the ground, unfortunately, not a lot has yet changed. There is talk about 99-year leases on land, but when you look at the small print, those 99-year leases are actually only 90-day leases, and there is a clause that allows government to cancel those leases with no notice in 90-days' time.

We are seeing talk about the rule of law coming back, property rights coming back, but at this stage, we have seen no laws actually changed. Even the Indigenization Act has not been repealed. We see the militarization of many parts of government. We have obviously got the former Minister of State Security as the President. We have got the former Minister of Defence, and after that, of the Armed Forces, as the Vice President. We have got the guy who was in charge of Fifth Brigade that massacred 20,000 people in Matabeleland as the Minister of Lands. And then, within the civil service, there are many military figures actually coming in, and within the Zimbabwe Electoral Commission as well.

So we have got a situation where there is a huge amount of charm, but we have still got the same situation on the ground. So I think we have to look at that, and we have to look at what needs to be done in order to restore rule of law and to restore property rights.

And I think ZDERA was a very far-thinking program or act that was put in place in December 2001, and I would like to recommend very strongly that ZDERA does remain in place. One of the aspects of ZDERA was respect for ownership and title to property, one of the main issues relating to the destruction of the economy.

And I believe that the judgment that came in from the SADC Tribunal, an African solution to an African problem, this tribunal that gave judgment in favor of property rights back in 2008, that should be incorporated within ZDERA so that it becomes the international legal obligations, as per the SADC treaty, should be brought in as part of ZDERA.

I think also we have talked a lot about free and fair elections. It is absolutely imperative that there are people on the ground observing now as to what is taking place in terms of the militarization of ZEC, the Zimbabwe Electoral Commission, and of the intimidation that is going on in the rural areas ahead of the election. And I think the third thing that is so important is that the SADC Tribunal, this court that was set up for the 280 million people in Southern Africa, is brought back into being. And at this stage we have done an awful lot. We are actually expecting a judgment tomorrow in South Africa regarding our case against President Zuma for his part in destroying that SADC Tribunal, and we expect a good judgment.

But we need to have other governments being brought to task within the SADC region, or other heads of state, for their part in signing a new protocol that takes away the rights of the individual to be able to go to that court as a court of last resort.

We hope for a better country, and I think a major step has been taken with President Mugabe not being in place any longer at the head. But we need the next step to be taken where the rule of law is brought back, where democracy is able to take place, and where human rights are respected along with property rights.

I thank you.

[The prepared statement of Mr. Freeth follows:]

U.S. CONGRESS: House Subcommittee on Africa hearing:
"The Recommended Focus of Future U.S. – Zimbabwe Relations"

By Ben Freeth, Executive Director,
Mike Campbell Foundation

28 February 2018

We need to get the root of the problem in Zimbabwe:

- What is it that caused the fastest shrinking economy in the recorded history of the world in a peace time situation?
- What is it that brought the most industrialized country in sub-Saharan Africa - after South Africa - into a state of 85% plus unemployment?
- What is it that made the bread basket of southern Africa into a country that would have had widespread death by starvation if food aid had not come in from the U.S. and the West every year for 16 years after the farm invasions began? For example, in 2002, just two years into the chaotic farm grab, Western governments had to give the World Food Program $300 million to feed some 5.5 million Zimbabweans, nearly 50% of the country's population. (At the height of the Ethiopian famine, international donors fed just 20% of Ethiopia's citizens.)[1]
- What is that has caused an estimated 25% of the entire Zimbabwe population of between 12 and 13 million people to flee the country of their birth in such a short period of time?

Most critically:

How can Zimbabwe be rebuilt from the ruins that have been created by the 37 years of former President Robert Mugabe's reign?

THE RECOMMENDED FOCUS FOR FUTURE U.S. – ZIMBABWE RELATIONS

The U.S. needs to focus on the current drive by Zimbabwe's leaders to bring in investment and financial aid given that some of the extremely negative and counterproductive laws, policies and practices remain in place. The Zimbabwe Democracy and Economic Recovery Act of 2001 (ZDERA)[2], passed by the U.S. Congress in December 2001, stipulates that the restoration of the rule of law in Zimbabwe includes *"respect for ownership and title to property."* [Section 4 (d)(1)]

Restoration and expansion of property rights

Commercial agriculture, underpinned by property rights, has always been the backbone of the economy. Prior to 2000, the year the farm invasions began, commercial agriculture with titled land accounted for approximately 30% of the land area of Zimbabwe.

This accounted for 20% of Zimbabwe's GDP, which rose to 60% when agri-based industries, including services, came into the equation. It also accounted for over 40% of national export earnings.

In addition, over 20 percent of the population lived and was employed on commercial farms, with commercial agriculture-related employment comprising a third of the formal labour force[3]. The destruction of property rights and the nationalisation of the vast majority of titled land has been catastrophic for the economy. On that nationalised land, no dams have been built, nor any meaningful development undertaken since the date of nationalisation. In fact, the vast majority of irrigation schemes have fallen into disuse, thousands of hectares of valuable forex-earning orchards have died, and thorn trees have begun to take over in many of the agricultural fields.

Comparison: (Left) Communal land vs (right) property-rights titled land in 2005
(Credit: National Geographic Society)

There is no doubt that if property rights were restored and expanded, there could be a very quick recovery in the agricultural sector. This would bring massive employment, a huge inflow of desperately needed foreign currency, a return of skills lost through the mass exodus of skilled Zimbabweans, and a revival in the local downstream industries, 60% of which were primarily focused on agriculture.

Bankable, transferable and inheritable property rights now only exist on less than 10% of the total land area in Zimbabwe. As a result, virtually no development or meaningful production and employment is able to take place because no investment is secure and nobody can take a long-term view – something essential for agriculture. Former commercial farms have become as unproductive as - or even less productive than their communal neighbours. A system of feudal patronage has developed throughout the land where everyone lives in fear, insecurity and poverty for the purposes of being easily controlled.

Three steps need to be taken to free the land, unlock its potential and bring it to life so that the remarkable human capital that Zimbabwe has available at its disposal can get involved with development, production and employment on the land:

1. Property rights need to be re-established in the recently nationalised commercial land [approximately 11 million hectares].
2. Property rights need to be re-established in the formerly nationalised commercial land that was bought by government for resettlement but on which no formal bankable or transferable property rights were given [3.6 million hectares].
3. Property rights need to be established for the first time in the communal areas [17 million hectares].

It is interesting to look at the country where the land nationalisation ideology that has been used in Zimbabwe originally came from. A little over a century ago, the great Russian Prime Minister and courageous reformer, Stolypin, began reforming the communal lands of Russia to give individual ownership to over 6 million peasant households in a decade. This increased total agricultural production by 50% in that decade because with individual ownership came development on those farms. Stolypin was murdered.

When Lenin took over immediately afterwards, he began his "command economy" and the peasants who had ownership had their property rights taken away with the infamous "land decree". With property rights destroyed, Russians starved by the million, despite having such a vast agricultural land area on which they could have fed the world.

Every land nationalisation program carried out around the world since Lenin's land decree of 26 October 1917, has had equally disastrous effects.

It is interesting to note that in line with the Leninist nationalisation in Zimbabwe, Zimbabwe has also instituted "command agriculture," mirroring Lenin's "command economy". The State commands and controls farmers in terms of whether they can grow and what they grow, as well as where they must market their produce. Last year the State paid farmers double the world price for maize and sold it on for half what they bought it for. This helped lead to a good harvest; but a record loss by the Grain Marketing Board of over 200 million dollars. Such madcap schemes from a cash-strapped government and a cash-strapped people who have to pay for such schemes, are totally unsustainable.

One of the sons of the Zimbabwean soil, Allan Savory - a visionary and a man very influential in world agriculture, including in the U.S., once said: "Without agriculture it is not possible to have a city, stock market, banks, university, church or army. Agriculture is the foundation of civilisation and any stable economy."

To be successful, agriculture has to be founded on secure, bankable and transferable property rights. The current 99-year leases with the clause that government can cancel them in 90 days, are simply perpetuating the problem of dead capital.

If we are able to marry the resurrection of currently dead land capital to the resurrection of effectively dead human capital, Zimbabwe would become the fastest growing economy in the world in a very short period of time.

Section 72 of the new Constitution (2013)

The primary focus initially needs to be on Section 72[4] of the Zimbabwe Constitution (2013) which was struck down in its previous form (as Amendment 17 to the previous Constitution) by the Campbell Judgment[5] in the SADC Tribunal. We need to ensure that this Judgment does not continue to be ignored.

[Amendment 17 was added to Zimbabwe's Constitution on September 14, 2005 to vest ownership of certain categories of land on the Zimbabwean government and to eliminate the courts' jurisdiction to hear any challenge to the land acquisitions. Commercial farmer Mike Campbell initiated proceedings in court on May 15, 2006, challenging the validity of Amendment 17.]

IN THE SOUTHERN AFRICAN DEVELOPMENT
COMMUNITY (SADC) TRIBUNAL

Case no. 02/2007

HELD AT WINDHOEK

In the matter between:

MIKE CAMPBELL (PRIVATE) LIMITED — First Applicant

WILLIAM MICHAEL CAMPBELL — Second Applicant

and

ROBERT GABRIEL MUGABE N.O.
IN HIS CAPACITY AS THE PRESIDENT OF ZIMBABWE — Respondent

Mike Campbell takes on President Robert Mugabe at the SADC Tribunal in Namibia in 2007

Section 72 allows the Zimbabwe Government to acquire any right or interests in private land by notice in the Gazette after which that land vests in the State with full title. "No compensation is payable in respect of its acquisition..." [Section 72(3)(a)]. "The acquisition may not be challenged on the grounds that it was discriminatory..." Section 72(3)(c). "An act of Parliament may make it an offence for any person, without lawful authority to possess or occupy agricultural land..."

The SADC Tribunal Judgment is a final and binding judgment. Section 72 is an anathema to human rights and the rule of law and will continue to stifle investment so long as it is not changed. No moves are being made to even discuss the removal of Section 72 – which is in conflict with the rest of the Zimbabwe Constitution - and the continued contempt of the Zimbabwe Government to the Campbell Judgment which strikes it down. Section 72 goes against the SADC Treaty, international law and all the human rights charters that Zimbabwe is signed up to.

If the new Zimbabwe Government was to decide to comply with the court orders that President Mugabe chose to defy (instead of continuing to be in contempt of court)[6] and the Campbell Judgment was to be recognised, there would be no stronger or better signal that investment and financial assistance could now pour into Zimbabwe. This would be the clearest possible signal to herald significant and immediate recovery of the agricultural sector and the economy as a whole.

Until the Zimbabwe Government complies with the court orders – and does so publicly - it is important that financial institutions and governments continue to raise the issue as a prerequisite for normalisation of relations and financial assistance.

Restoration of the rule of law

At the root of the Zimbabwe problem is the breakdown of the rule of law and its replacement with "rule by law." We have a "command economy" with a military system of command in Government.

We have already covered the **Campbell farm case** in relation to Section 72 of the Constitution. My father-in-law, Mike Campbell, was abducted and severely beaten – and later died because he took President Mugabe to court in the regional court, the SADC Tribunal. This is what has happened in the past to those standing for the rule of law. Mike gained a final and binding judgment from the Tribunal in November 2008.[7] This needs to be recognised and adhered to.

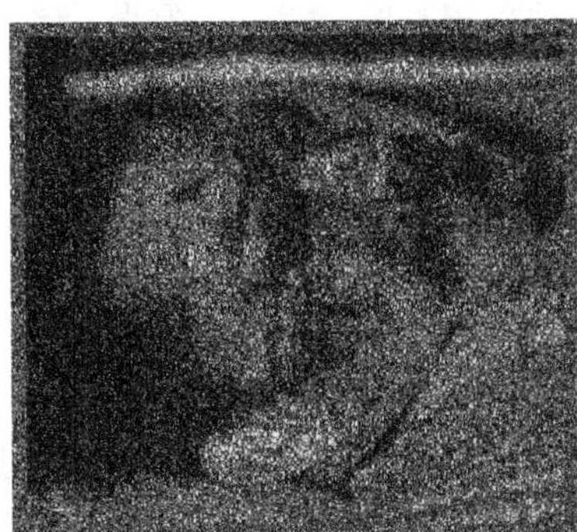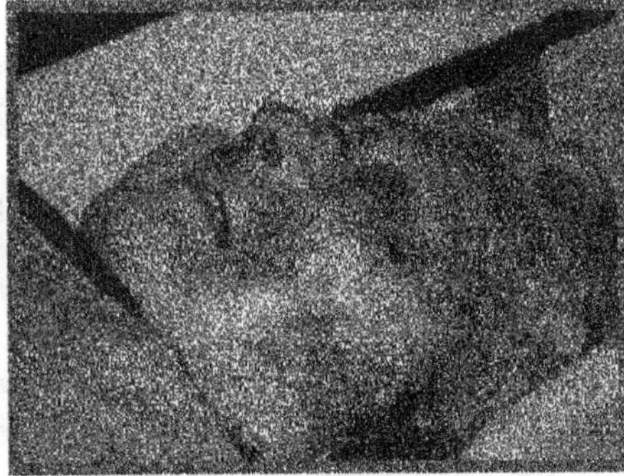

(Left): Ben Freeth and Mike Campbell in hospital after their abduction and torture at the hands of President Mugabe's youth militia, 30 June 2008

The Gondo torture case: In January 2011, the SADC Tribunal awarded damages of nearly US$17 million to nine Zimbabwean torture victims, in a landmark ruling that yet again exposed Harare's flagrant disregard of the rule of law. The judgment in the Gondo case[8], which was handed down on 9 December 2010, followed a case in which the victims of organised violence and torture sued the Zimbabwean government for failing to comply with the orders of the country's High Court.

After the Zimbabwe Government was found to be in contempt of court in the Campbell case, and the ruling of the Tribunal in the Gondo case was handed down, Mugabe managed to persuade the SADC Heads of State to suspend the SADC Tribunal in May 2011. The following year the SADC Heads of State closed down the Tribunal, depriving 277 million people in the 15 countries in southern Africa of a court of last resort when the justice systems in their own countries failed them.

The decision to do this and attempt to sign a new Protocol into place in 2014, the mandate of which would be confined to interpretation of the SADC Treaty and Protocols relating to *disputes between Member States*, thus blocking the Tribunal from hearing any human rights cases at all, is currently being challenged in the region. I am one of the applicants in a case against former South African President Jacob Zuma[9] for his part in the process. We expect a judgment before the date of this Congressional Hearing.

Other Laws: Detrimental laws remain in place despite lip service to their removal.

- The Indigenisation and Economic Empowerment Act of 2008[10] effectively stops white Zimbabweans or foreign investors from having a controlling share in any business;
- The Gazetted Land (Consequential Provisions) Act of 2006[11] continues to prosecute white farmers criminally for still farming their land and living in their homes as per Section 72 of the 2013 Constitution;
- The Public Order and Security Act (POSA)[12] of January 2002 and
- The Access to Information and Protection of Privacy Act (AIPPA)[13] of 2002 continue to stifle fundamental freedoms.

There is only one case where a white farmer has been restored to his farm. Rob Smart, his son Darryn and their families were evicted violently by police last year after a bishop, reportedly connected to former first lady Grace Mugabe's 'G40' political faction, was given the farm.

Regrettably Rob Smart's restoration is against Zimbabwe law as it now stands. The court order that evicted him has not been revoked and nothing has yet been put in place to change the law that led to his eviction. This demonstrates how we live in a rule by decree State. Laws need to be reformed so that violence against people and their property is able to be curbed.

[The Smarts have been told they will get a 99-year lease where, having received no compensation for their farm - which is now considered State land - they can lease their homes and land back from the State for an as yet unspecified amount of money each year. In the convoluted 48-page 99-year lease agreement, the State can evict the lessee with 90 days notice – even if he has crops in the ground].

Farm workers and their children were overjoyed when commercial farmers Darryn Smart and his father, Rob, were allowed to return to their Lesbury farm in December 2017

The U.S. continues to play a crucial role in Zimbabwe

America's values continue to guide foreign policy in Zimbabwe by supporting democratic movements and human rights organizations, as well as contributing very significantly to humanitarian projects.

We are deeply grateful to the U.S. for continuing to post exceptional diplomats such as former Ambassador James D. McGee to Harare. Ambassador McGee was prepared to risk his life by going out to witness state-sponsored violence against Zimbabweans in the rural areas first-hand - with the press.

 On February 24, 2009 shortly after the swearing in of Zimbabwe's Government of National Unity, Ambassador McGee addressed students at the African University in Mutare. His words apply equally today to the new government led by President Emmerson Mnangagwa:

"Despite all the challenges I remain hopeful that true change is coming. I hope that the new [unity] government represents a beginning. We are watching closely and will judge this new government on its actions. If it takes concrete steps to meet the conditions the international community laid out long ago for re-engagement, the United States will be at the forefront in providing assistance.

"However before that can happen, we need to see restoration of the rule of law, commitment to the democratic process and respect for human rights, a commitment to timely and internationally supervised elections, full and equal access for all Zimbabweans to humanitarian assistance, and commitment to macroeconomic stabilization in accordance with guidance from relevant international agencies. An important and necessary first step is the release of all political detainees. If we see signs that this is taking place our support will expand. If we do not see these signs, we will continue to provide humanitarian relief while pushing for these changes...."

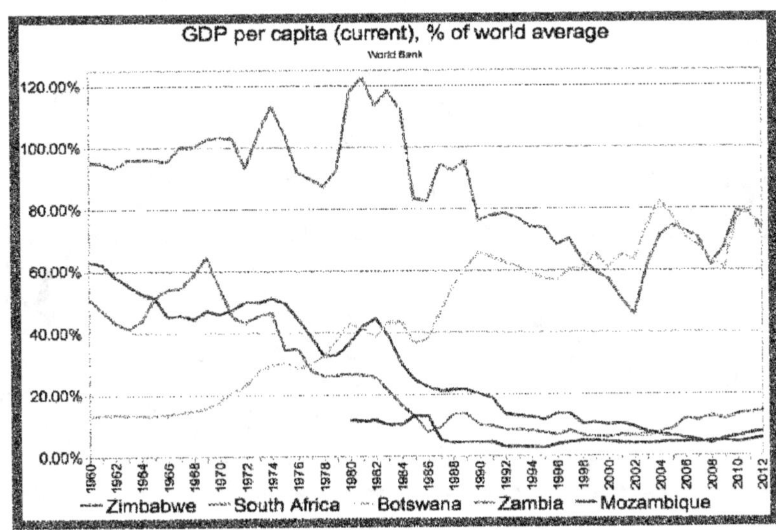

Zimbabwe's GDP per capita, compared to neighbouring countries, 1990-2012

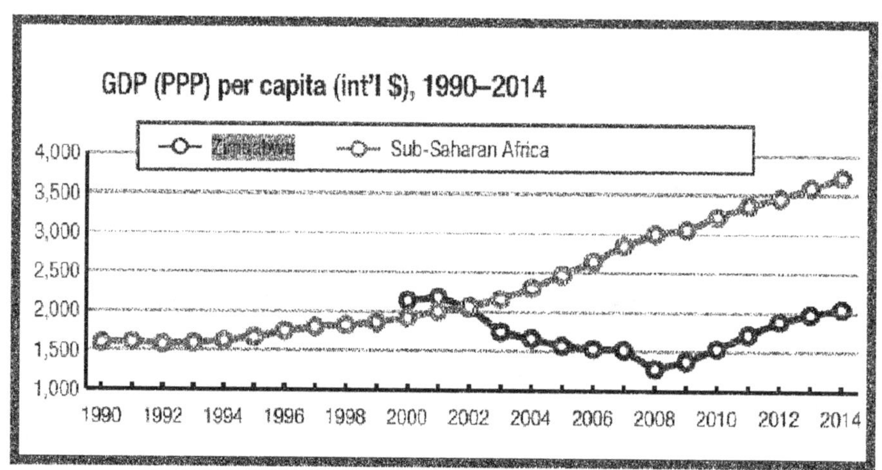

Zimbabwe's GDP (PPP) per capita compared to sub-Saharan Africa, 1990-2014
World Economic Forum
http://www3.weforum.org/docs/gcr/2015-2016/Global_Competitiveness_Report_2015-2016.pdf

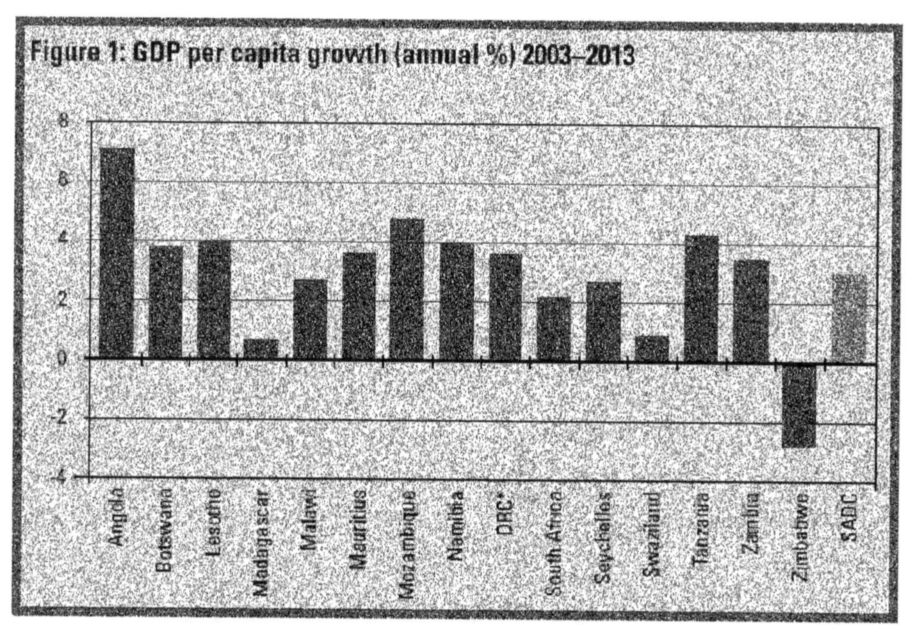

Source: World Bank, *World Development Indicators*, http://data.worldbank.org/data-catalog/worlddevelopment-indicators, accessed 22 October 2014

Ben Freeth MBE
Executive Director
Mike Campbell Foundation – Zimbabwe   Website: www.mikecampbellfoundation.com
Mobile: +263 773 929 138 E-mail: benfreeth7@gmail.com; info@mikecampbellfoundation.com

[1] "How to Kill a Country" by Samantha Power, The Atlantic, December 2003:
https://www.theatlantic.com/magazine/archive/2003/12/how-to-kill-a-country/302845/

[2] The Zimbabwe Democracy and Economic Recovery Act of 2001 (ZDERA)
https://www.congress.gov/107/plaws/publ99/PLAW-107publ99.pdf

[3] "Agriculture: The tale of Zimbabwe's sleeping giant" by NewsDay, 19 September 2013:
https://www.newsday.co.zw/2013/09/agriculture-tale-zimbabwes-sleeping-giant/

[4] Section 72 of the new Zimbabwean Constitution of 2103, analysis by Dr Dale Doré, 10 March 2013:
http://www.thezimbabwean.co/2013/03/the-good-the-bad-and/

[5] Mike Campbell (Pvt) Ltd v Zimbabwe, case summary on Wikipedia:
https://en.wikipedia.org/wiki/Mike_Campbell_(Pvt)_Ltd_v_Zimbabwe

Mike Campbell (Pvt) Ltd v Zimbabwe, background and rulings:
http://www.mikecampbellfoundation.com/page/the-campbell-case-background-rulings-461

[6] "The Zimbabwe Government remains in contempt of court and continues to flout the rule of law", opinion by Sir Jeffrey Jowell QC, The Zimbabwean, 18 May 2017:
http://www.thezimbabwean.co/2017/05/zimbabwe-government-remains-contempt-court-continues-flout-rule-law/

[7] Mike Campbell (Pvt) Ltd v Zimbabwe, judgment, South African Legal Information Institute, 2008:
http://www.saflii.org/sa/cases/SADCT/2008/2.html

[8] The Gondo torture case judgment, World Courts website, 9 December 2010:
http://www.worldcourts.com/sadct/eng/decisions/2010.12.09_Gondo_v_Zimbabwe.htm

[9] Hearing of SADC Tribunal court case set down for 5-7 February 2018, PoliticsWeb, 2 February 2018:
http://www.politicsweb.co.za/politics/hearing-of-sadc-tribunal-case-set-down-for-5-to-7-

[10] The Indigenisation and Economic Empowerment Act of 2008, Pindula website, 2008:
https://www.pindula.co.zw/Indigenisation_and_Economic_Empowerment_in_Zimbabwe

[11] The Gazetted Land (Consequential Provisions) Act of 2006, Zimbabwe Legal Information Institute:
https://www.zimlii.org/zw/legislation/num-
act/2006/8/Gazetted%20Land%20%28Consequential%20Provisions%29%20Act%20%282006%29%20%281%29.pdf

[12] The Public Order and Security Act (POSA) of January 2002: Solidarity Peace Trust Report "Policing the State", summary on pg 4, 14 December 2016:
http://solidaritypeacetrust.org/download/report-files/policing_the_state.pdf

[13] The Access to Information and Protection of Privacy Act of 2002: Wikipedia:
https://en.wikipedia.org/wiki/Access_to_Information_and_Protection_of_Privacy_Act_(Zimbabwe)

Mr. SMITH. Thank you so very much, Mr. Freeth.

We now go to our fourth and final panelist, Dr. Dendere.

Thank you again for being here.

STATEMENT OF CHIPO DENDERE, PH.D., VISITING ASSISTANT PROFESSOR, AMHERST COLLEGE

Ms. DENDERE. Thank you, Chairman Smith and Ranking Member Karen Bass, for the invitation to testify today.

The United States and Zimbabwe have had a long and supportive relationship. The United States remains Zimbabwe's biggest donor and has already given $1 billion in aid since 2001.

The ouster of Mr. Mugabe in November 2017 after a military-led guardian coup that ended in his resignation is an outcome that many of us would not have predicted. I believe I also speak for my generation, those of us born after independence, when I say the idea of a post-Mugabe Zimbabwe is quite surreal.

Mr. Mugabe's 37-year tenure was complex. While he made significant improvements in welfare provisions, his authoritarian rule resulted in much suffering, notably, the 1983 Matabeleland genocide and violence again political opponents.

In response to the declining economy, at least 2 million Zimbabweans emigrated. At least 80,000 of those found refuge in the United States. Zimbabweans in the United States are highly skilled and many of them have been educated at top universities, including MIT, Harvard, and Yale.

Zimbabwean Americans have also made significant contributions in the arts. For example, the brilliant "Black Panther" actress Danai Gurira.

While Zimbabweans celebrated the change in the government, this quickly turned into allowing the continued involvement of the military in otherwise civilian affairs. When I flew into the Harare International Airport in early December, soldiers required everyone arriving to show our IDs. This was new for Zimbabwe.

It is unlikely that an unreformed ZANU-PF government will usher in a democratic system. It is also unlikely, following the death of Morgan Tsvangirai, that a divided opposition climate will spread democratic growth.

It is my expert opinion that additional government-to-government aid and investment will not solve Zimbabwe's problems in the absence of significant reforms that address elections, corruption, and economic development.

While President Mnangagwa has stated his commitment to free and fair elections, state media is heavily controlled by the ruling party. Democracy cannot thrive when the media is stifled. State institutions such as the police and the military remain partisan. The peacefulness of the 2018 election is thus at risk.

Zimbabwe's high youth unemployment has also created a readily available marketplace of youth who can be paid to harm others. Interparty violence is also a growing concern.

However, despite the restricted access to state media, initiatives such as the Open Parly platform and BusStopTV, a political satire group, have effectively utilized social media and have a combined reach of over ½ million citizens.

Voice of America remains an important media platform, reaching nearly 700,000 citizens weekly. I recommend that the United States continue providing funding for VOA and independent media. Zimbabwe loses between $1 billion to $2 billion from corruption each year. President Mnangagwa has promised zero tolerance of corruption. However, to date, corruption investigations have targeted only those affiliated with the losing pro-Mugabe faction of ZANU-PF. At least five members of President Mnangagwa's cabinet have been implicated in corruption worth billions of dollars.

Although President Mnangagwa recently announced that some officials have heeded his call to return stolen funds and to declare assets, no specifics have been shared about those returns.

Corruption is an epidemic. For this reason, it is important for the United States to engage the new government very strongly and firmly on corruption.

ZANU-PF often blamed Zimbabwe's stunted economic growth on economic sanctions, in particular the United States' Zimbabwe Democracy and Economic Recovery Act, ZDERA. Lack of clarity on both the Zimbabwe and U.S. investor side on the requirements of ZDERA have had some negative implications on investment.

For example, Zimbabwean businesses have been denied credit by American banks who are not clear on the policy requirements under ZDERA. Clarity on the types of business-to-business engagements acceptable within the confines of ZDERA is required.

I also recommend that the United States reconsider sanctions on state-owned businesses. Justifiably, the United States has long been concerned with the links between ZANU-PF and state enterprises. Indeed, much of the corruption has occurred in the state-owned businesses.

However, it is my expert opinion that in the post-Mugabe era, legislative independence has been bolstered and the Parliament is now equipped to hold government officials to account.

Regarding individual sanctions, the onus is on those listed to prove their commitment to democracy. Many on the list have allegedly committed horrible crimes against humanity. It would be a greater injustice to lift these sanctions before a thorough investigation has been conducted. Zimbabwe cannot have economic growth that is divorced from addressing human rights abuses.

Robert Mugabe's exit from politics is not enough to absolve individual crimes. President Mnangagwa's motto is that Zimbabwe is open for business. Zimbabwe has long been open for business, but poor governance bottlenecked efforts by local and foreign investors.

President Mnangagwa has said all the right things necessary for a conducive business environment in Zimbabwe. The real test will be whether he follows through on his promises. His government has thus far made adjustments to unpopular policies, including the Indigenization and Empowerment Act, which should help increase investor confidence.

While the United States faces tough competition from China and Russia in sourcing Zimbabwe's natural resources, Zimbabweans that I have spoken to have indicated a preference for American business. A democratic Zimbabwe and strengthened U.S.-Zimbabwe economic partnership remains mutually beneficial for the two countries.

Thank you.
[The prepared statement of Ms. Dendere follows:]

Testimony of Dr. Chipo Dendere
Consortium for Faculty Diversity Fellow & Visiting Assistant Professor of Political Science,
Amherst College
House Foreign Affairs Committee
Subcommittee on Africa, Global Health and Human Rights
February 28, 2018

Chipo Dendere is a Zimbabwean political scientist. Dr. Dendere is currently a Consortium for Faculty Diversity Fellow and Visiting Assistant Professor of Political Science at Amherst College. Dr. Dendere's research expertise is on democracy, elections, and, migration, with a regional focus on African politics. She writes about the impact of voter exit, migration and remittances on the survival of authoritarian regimes. Dr. Dendere's new research is on the role of technology and social media in new democracies.

Thank you, Chairman Christopher H. Smith, Ranking Member Karen Bass and other members of the Subcommittee, for the invitation to testify today on the future of Zimbabwe in a post-Robert Mugabe era. As a scholar of African politics, I can say that this is an outcome many of us would not have predicted. I believe I speak for most young Zimbabweans, my generation born after independence, when I say the idea of a post-Mugabe Zimbabwe is quite surreal.

Robert Mugabe was ousted from office in November 2017 in a series of military-led events that began as a guardian coup resulting in his resignation.

The United States and Zimbabwe have a long history of a mutually beneficial and productive relationship. In 1980, the United States was the first country to open an embassy in the newly independent Zimbabwe and extended a state visit invitation to then Prime Minister Robert Mugabe.[1] Over the last two decades as Zimbabwe faced severe economic and political crises, the relationship has been strained, but the United States has remained committed to providing support for democracy and alleviating poverty. The United States remains the biggest donor and has given nearly USD$1 billion dollars in foreign assistance since 2001.[2] In 2001, the United States Congress passed the Zimbabwe Democracy and Economic Recovery Act (ZIDERA),[3] commonly referred to as *sanctions* in Zimbabwe. Mugabe and his government blamed many of the countries' economic woes on these sanctions. Debates on sanctions are complex, and there is a lot of academic evidence that suggests sanctions negatively affect the poorest and most vulnerable. At the same time, targeted sanctions also constrain the behavior of rogue politicians who would otherwise have free access to resources around the world while denying their own citizens the same opportunities.

It is my goal in this testimony to provide a broader political and economic context of Zimbabwe post-Mugabe and give some suggestions on future engagement that will bolster political stability and democratic consolidation. It is unlikely that the new ZANU PF government will usher in a democratic system that alleviates poverty and respects civil liberties. It is also unlikely following the death of key opposition figure Morgan Tsvangirai that the opposition will spur democratic growth. At the heart of Zimbabwe's democratic challenges in the post-Mugabe era is debilitating poverty. In the absence of rigorous efforts to address high unemployment rates, poor health care and violence, Zimbabwe's democratic future remains grim.

Background on Zimbabwe
Zimbabwe gained independence in 1980 after almost two decades of protracted war between black nationalists and a white minority government. At independence, Robert Mugabe who was then Prime Minister made a public promise to uphold democracy. President Mugabe's 37-year tenure was complex: while his government made significant improvements in welfare provision and universal access to education, his authoritarian rule also resulted in much suffering, notably the 1983 genocide in Matabeleland and targeted violence against the opposition led by the recently deceased Mr. Tsvangirai. In the early 2000s, the economy went into rapid decline, in part because of failed

---

[1] U.S. Department of State, "Zimbabwe."

[2] U.S. Department of State, "U.S. Foreign Aid to Zimbabwe."

[3] William Bill Frist, Zimbabwe Democracy and Economic Recovery Act (ZIDERA).

governance, a poorly executed land reform policy, sanctions and state sponsored violence on citizens and the opposition.

The declining economic and political conditions in Zimbabwe led to a massive exodus of an estimated 2-4 million Zimbabweans who sought refuge abroad. An estimated 80,000 Zimbabweans found refuge in the United States. The Zimbabwean immigrant population is highly skilled and makes significant contributions to the United States economy, many of them having been educated at top universities including The Massachusetts Institute of Technology (MIT), Harvard and Yale. Zimbabwean-Americans have also made their mark in the arts, including, for example, the brilliant Black Panther actress Danai Gurira.

Current political climate

Zimbabwe is headed towards elections in a few months. President Mnangagwa who succeeded Robert Mugabe is eager to move past elections and has hinted at an early election, likely in July. Zimbabwe is going through a delicate transition following the military-assisted removal of Robert Mugabe from office by then Vice President Mnangagwa in November 2017. Mugabe's ouster from office marked the first change in power since independence. Although Zimbabwe's process differed from traditional coups in Africa that were bloody and violent, it was not a wholesome democratic transition either, as President Mnangagwa did not become president via the ballot box.

Drawing on more than 30 extensive interviews conducted with elites and ordinary citizens during and after the coup I observed that while Zimbabweans celebrate and welcome the change in government, people remain concerned about the visible presence of the military in everyday politics. President Mnangagwa appears to have rewarded the military by appointing former generals to top government positions. Former Generals who played significant roles in the military takeover, Constantino Chiwenga and Sibusiso Moyo, were appointed Vice President and Minister of Foreign Affairs respectively. When I flew into the Harare International Airport in early December, soldiers asked me and everyone else arriving to show our IDs. This is new for Zimbabwe. The presence of the military stood in stark contrast to the eerie absence of the police. During Mugabe's tenure, Zimbabwe had become a heavily policed state, with police roadblocks every few meters and commonplace police demands for bribes poor motorists.

While a lot of challenges remain, I have also noticed that since November 2017, Zimbabweans are more hopeful. Following President Mnangagwa's inauguration, we saw the celebrated return of prominent exiles. Among these is the anticipated return of famous musician Thomas Mapfumo. In December we also saw the return of some white farmers who had sought exile abroad after the land reform process turned violent. An estimated 4,000 white farmers and their black farm workers were displaced in the early 2000s.[4] It is very unlikely that the "new" ZANU PF will reverse land reform, but President Mnangagwa has promised a more progressive and inclusive policy.

Generally, Zimbabweans are more confident to speak out, although many worry that the new government will restrict freedom of speech at the slightest hint that its hold on power is under threat. It is my expert opinion that once people have found their voice, it is a lot harder for governments to shut them down. This shift in citizen attitudes provides a unique opportunity for the United States and other friends of Zimbabwe to empower the average citizen.

---

[4] "White Farmer Gets Land Back under Zimbabwe's New Leader."

Challenges and opportunities in a post-Mugabe society

In my interviews, Zimbabweans expressed that they are tired of being a global agenda item for the wrong reasons. Zimbabweans are eager to get back to the business of rebuilding their country and bringing back dignity. Most feel that a post-Mugabe era will open doors for development. This sentiment is shared by a lot of investors and donor countries who have been quick to extend a helping hand to the new government.

While I share the hope of many Zimbabweans, it is my expert opinion that additional aid and investment will not solve Zimbabwe's problems in the absence of significant reforms to reduce poverty and strengthen institutions. If President Mnangagwa's government or the next government that wins in elections in 2018 does not address deeply entrenched corruption, violation of various human rights, including property rights and punitive economic policies the United States, other donors and investors will not see positive returns on their investments. Investment partners are likely to see better returns on their efforts if they shift from government-to-government partnerships and focus on engaging at the local level, supporting entrepreneurs, local businesses, independent media houses and civil society.

The political environment: is Zimbabwe ready for elections?

On February 26, 2018, Zimbabwe's Election Commission chair announced that elections would be held between July and August 2018. At least 5.3 million out of the 7 million eligible voters have registered to vote. Among those registered, the majority, some 65%, are youth. There is no indication that the new government will put in place substantial electoral reforms to even out the playing field but that does not mean that the country is not ready for elections. In the last 18 years Zimbabwean politics has been very tumultuous. And yet, the opposition has made significant strides even winning the 2008 election.

Factors that will have a major impact on the elections include access to free media, youth bulge, and violence:

Media

State media is heavily controlled by the ruling party but there are new opportunities for independent coverage via social media. Zimbabwe has one television channel that is state run. The main newspaper, the *Herald*, is also state-run and provides partisan coverage. Democracy cannot thrive when the media is stifled. There are also a number of independent media house in circulation including the daily news but they have limited resources. While the environment is certainly challenging, entrepreneurial youth have taken advantage of the growing access to social media to provide citizens with alternative sources for news. One example is the #openparly platform founded Youth African Leaders Initiative (YALI) alumni their social media platforms reach at least 200,000 citizens daily. Another independent media source is BusStopTV, a political satire group that has a reach of over half a million on their popular segments. The United States Embassy has already begun efforts to provide funding for these informal news outlets and should continue to do so.

Voice of America remains an important media platform. In the most recent survey conducted in 2015, VOA's past-week reach in Zimbabwe stood at 5.8%, an impressive figure in a market which limits access to international broadcasters. In a more recent qualitative study conducted in 2017, Zimbabweans reported that VOA delivers unique content because it broadcasts information that they are unable to get elsewhere. In addition, VOA's coverage of political news is not biased or censored like the local news. As long as censorship continues in Zimbabwe, panelists feel that VOA's Studio 7 will remain a valuable source of information. VOA's audience reach is steadily increasing because of their efforts to use social media platforms. I regularly engage with listeners as a panelist of VOA shows and I am happy to report that we receive calls from very diverse and often remote areas of Zimbabwe. I would recommend that the United States continue providing funding for VOA.

Youth, Unemployment, Political Violence and Restriction of civil liberties

While the President Mnangagwa has stated his commitment to a violent free election, the 2018 political climate may not be free and fair. Zimbabwe's high youth unemployment has created a readily available and cheap marketplace for young people who can be paid to harm others. Substance abuse that can be traced back to poverty and trauma caused by political instability is on the rise especially among recent graduates.

Between November and December 2017, the Counseling Services Unit, an NGO tasked with documenting incidents of political violence and providing care for the affected, reported 89 attacks on members of the opposition. The police continue to respond to public protests with excessive and needless violence. Intra and inter party violence is also a growing concern in Zimbabwe's "new dispensation."[5] Particularly troubling is violence targeting women. It is important to emphasize that the culture of violence is a result of years of authoritarianism and has been made worse by growing unemployment, citizen fatigue and a very harsh kind of poverty.

The challenge for ZANU PF and the opposition is that the perpetrators of violence-many of them youth- at the local level are unlikely to change their behavior and attitude toward political opponents unless there is direct commitment from all political actors to educate against political violence. Years of unstable governance have completely changed the political climate and social structures in Zimbabwe. In a country with a significant youth population serious efforts have to be made to manage political violence.

Zimbabwe has experienced a significant youth bulge. According to the 2013 census, the majority, 76%, of the population were under the age of 34. This presents both opportunities and challenges for Zimbabwe. On one hand, Zimbabwe's youth are also highly educated and on the other hand most of the youth are unemployed or underemployed. Every year at least 2,000 young people graduate with a diverse range of degrees in Engineering, Business, Law, Math and Science. As Zimbabwe transitions, if the government partnerships with big trade partners like the United States yield significant economic gains, then the youth bulge will prove advantageous for Zimbabwe. As the economy grows, Zimbabwe's dependency ratio – the proportion of non-working population to working population- will decline. The United States government has already implemented numerous community-based programs that have had a positive impact on the youth. For example, the work readiness program "Zimbabwe:works" has generated over $31 million in revenue and created 6,000 jobs[6]. The Youth African Leaders Initiative (YALI) participants are some of the most active youth and leaders in job creation. Six of the youth "hub" or job centers were founded by Yali alumni; together they have created over 100 jobs in less than two years.

---

[5] "Zimbabwe: ZLHR Condemns MDC-T Intra-Party Violence - allAfrica.com."
[6] "Zimbabwe."

However, these efforts are not enough. At least 90% of Zimbabwe's youth are unemployed and this is a big challenge for democracy and peace. Youth are used by political parties to mobilize voters and to also terrorize voters. In my interviews, voters have expressed fear of party-affiliated youth who are easily lured by promises of small payments and access to drugs.

The United States can continue working with and within the civil society on youth targeted educational programs that promote peace and democracy. In 2017, the United States spent an estimated $158 million on health programs focused on HIV/AIDS, malaria, malnutrition, TB, maternal/child health, family planning, and water sanitation. These programs are critical and must continue. A healthier Zimbabwe creates important trade opportunities for the United States.

Corruption
At the heart of Zimbabwe's problems is endemic corruption. Zimbabwe loses between USD$1-2 billion from corruption each year.[7] To put that in perspective, Zimbabwe's annual budget hovers just above $4 billion. Zimbabwe is ranked in the top 30 most corrupt countries in the world.[8] In public opinion surveys conducted by Michigan University's Afrobaromter, at least 72% of Zimbabweans believe the majority of government officials to be corrupt., Perceived and real corruption scares serious investors away from Zimbabwe, creating opportunities for rogue businessmen who cause more harm from their business practices.

President Mnangagwa has promised zero tolerance of corruption. However, to date corruption investigations have targeted those affiliated with the G-40 faction of ZANU PF.[9] President Mnangagwa gave officials a February deadline to return any stolen funds and to declare assets. The President has said some officials have returned funds, but he has not shared any specifics about those returns. In his own administration, President Mnangagwa's has appointed individuals accused of corruption. Five of his cabinet members have been implicated in corruption worth billions of dollars[10].

In 2016, President Mugabe announced that Zimbabwe had lost USD$15 billion in diamond revenue to corruption. These numbers have not been verified but during a recent hearing on diamond revenues, the commission on diamonds revealed that they had expected at least USD$2 billion from diamonds sold since 2009. To date only $189 million had been tendered to the government between 2009-2016. A plurality (40%) of Zimbabweans believe that government officials in all sectors are corrupt.

As long as poverty is not addressed, corruption will continue to be an epidemic. Troubling incidents of dehumanization of vulnerable persons have been reported by the UNCHR, the over 19,000 refugees in Zimbabwe's camps are often forced to pay bribes to corrupt government officials in exchange for access to basic commodities. For this reason, it is important for the United States to engage the new government very strongly and firmly on corruption. The United States, must continue engaging in local level programs that can be insulated from government corruption. While

---

[7] "Zimbabwe Losing $1 Billion a Year to Corruption."

[8] "Transparency International - Zimbabwe."

[9] "Former Zimbabwe Ministers Loyal to Mugabe Charged with Corruption."

[10] "5 Ministers in Mnangagwa's cabinet that have been implicated in corruption scandals"

low level everyday citizen corruption exists, the cost of that type of corruption is minimal when compared to the value of money lost via government channels.

Economic Development

Robert Mugabe often blamed Zimbabe's stunted economic growth on economic sanctions in particular the United States' Zimbabwe Democracy and Economic Recovery Act (ZIDERA). Confusion on both the Zimbabwe and U.S. investor side on the requirements of ZIDERA has negatively impacted investment in Zimbabwe. Zimbabwean businesses have been denied loans by American banks who are not clear on the policy requirements under ZIDERA.

For most investors perception is reality. The fact that Zimbabwe is identified as a country under sanctions has scared away potential investors. I have recommended that the United States provide clarity on the types of business to business engagements acceptable within the confines of ZIDERA. I would also recommend that the United States support efforts by Zimbabweans asking for debt relief from international funding agencies including the World Bank and IMF. Such efforts will bring much needed relief to millions of Zimbabweans, especially farmers, who could increase food production if they have access to credit. Extending credit to startups can allow business owners like Simbarashe Mhuriro, 32, founder and Managing Director a renewable energy development company to employ more people thereby providing sustainable solutions to poverty. Addressing poverty will have a direct and positive impact on democratic growth in Zimbabwe.

With regards to individuals and government institutions under the targeted sanctions list, the post-Mugabe era provides new opportunities for engagement between Zimbabwe and the United States. I recommend that the United States reconsider sanctions on state owned businesses. I recognize that the United States has long been concerned with the link between ZANU PF and state enterprises. Indeed, much of the corruption I discussed earlier has occurred in state owned businesses. However, it is my expert opinion that in the post-Mugabe era parliament has been bolstered in their independence and are better equipped hold government officials account. I would like to draw attention to those parastatals engaged in agriculture and mining industries. Most small holder farmers depend heavily on funding from the state funded agriculture bank which in turn depends on support from big financial institutions.

State owned and other enterprises under targeted sanctions include:
AGRIBANK
INDUSTRIAL DEVELOPMENT CORPORATION OF ZIMBABWE LTD INFRASTRUCTURE
DEVELOPMENT BANK OF ZIMBABWE MINERALS MARKETING CORPORATION OF ZIMBABWE
ZB FINANCIAL HOLDINGS LIMITED
INTERMARKET HOLDINGS LIMITED
SCOTFIN LIMITED
ZIMBABWE IRON AND STEEL COMPANY
ZIMBABWE MINING DEVELOPMENT CORPORATION
ZIMRE HOLDINGS LIMITED
OSLEG (PVT) LTD
ORYX DIAMONDS (PTY) LTD
ZIMBABWE DEFENCE INDUSTRIES (PVT) LTD

Regarding individual sanctions; the onus is on those listed to prove their commitment to democracy. Many on the list have allegedly committed horrible crimes against humanity. It would be a greater injustice to uplift these sanctions before a thorough investigation has been conducted. Zimbabwe cannot have economic growth divorced from addressing human rights abuses. Robert Mugabe's exit from politics is not enough to absolve individual crimes.

President Mnangagwa's motto is "Zimbabwe is open for business". The truth is that Zimbabwe has long been open for business but poor governance bottlenecked efforts by investors. President Mnangagwa has said all the right things necessary for a conducive business environment in Zimbabwe. The real test will be whether he follows through on his promises. Since coming into power he has made few adjustments to unpopular policies including the 2016 Indigenization and Empowerment Act[11]. This amendment should increase investor confidence and woo American investors who had moved away from investing in Zimbabwe. While the United States faces tough competition from China and Russia in sourcing Zimbabwe's natural resources, average Zimbabweans I have spoken to over the last three months have a preference for American businesses. Little known is the extensive collaboration between American and Zimbabwean farmers. Increased investment in agriculture will provide much needed food security for both countries as the world faces troubling weather changes. Zimbabwe's high literacy rates also create important opportunities for American businesses seeking to expand their market and manufacturing basis. Such partnerships can bolster employment in both countries in exciting and mutually beneficial ways.

Conclusion

While Zimbabwe faces a long and hard road to economic and political recovery the current government and the government that wins the 2018 elections have the opportunity to change the narrative. The new government must implement reforms to open up political space and policies that will increase the ease of doing business and addressing corruption. A post-Mugabe Zimbabwe will not thrive if the government only focuses on the economy while ignoring the need for political reforms.

The United States also has an opportunity to revise some of the conditions of the Zimbabwe Democracy and Economic Recovery Act (ZIDERA). It is beneficial to the United States to provide clarity for American businesses working with Zimbabweans and to also support efforts by Zimbabweans seeking debt relief for their country. The Zimbabwean government should engage in extensive investigations on human rights abuses before individuals on the targeted list of sanctions have been removed.

The quality of the 2018 elections will determine the "new" ZANU PF's commitment to democracy. It is also clear that the average Zimbabwean is more hopeful than they have ever been and support for civil society organizations will bolster this support for democracy among regular citizens.

---

[11] "Govt Amends Indigenisation Law | The Herald."

Mr. SMITH. Thank you. I thought you might have had one final statement to make. I appreciate it.

Let me begin the questioning. First, maybe, Ambassador Ray, if I go to you, but others who would like to answer these questions, please do.

We know that Mnangagwa was obviously head of state security and the CIO during some very, very brutal periods, hence, the name "crocodile," perhaps, but also people would suggest that maybe he is a changed man today.

It is important to know, past sometimes is prologue. Far too often it is prologue. I wonder, however, how many political prisoners years-to-date have there been in Zimbabwe?

And if you could expound upon the use of torture. I have authored four laws on torture victims. It is called the Torture Victims Relief Act. And here in this room I have heard testimony, as has my staff, as well as in countries all over the world, at torture centers, as well as in prisons, the Laogai, in Jakarta, the Soviet Union. The use of torture is often endemic.

And Mr. Freeth—and, without objection, your full statement, like all of your full statements, will be made a part of the record—you have a picture of both you and Mike Campbell, your father-in-law, who was killed by way of a beating, and you with blood all over your face. And you point out, obviously, that will be another question, about the SADC courts—and, Ambassador, you might want to speak to that as well—which were done away with in 2012.

Is that something that would come back? Is that something that the Trump administration and the European Community and especially the African countries need to say that needs to be returned. Legacy human rights issues are as important as current day human rights issues. There is no statute of limitations on torture and other kinds of horrific misdeeds or murder.

So if you could speak to that, if you would, as an opening.

And then I have some additional questions about the Dr. Frist-Feingold legislation, which we have already heard a lot of talk about, ZDERA, that had to do, obviously, with loans and no more debt relief. And you may recall debt relief during those years was one of the most popular issues around. Bono certainly helped to make it very popular. But debt relief is off the table when you are dealing within an abuser, abusing country.

I think, Mr. Freeth, you at least alluded to or maybe you even said how important it was that SADC restoration, especially judgments, ought to be part of lifting of sanctions. And maybe you want to speak to that as well.

Ambassador RAY. All right. Thank you, sir.

As to the number of prisoners, I am afraid I don't know—either currently or historically, I don't know currently and historically, if I was told. I have reached an age where my brain cells don't retain such things.

On the issue of the SADC Tribunal, I would strongly suggest that we reach out to whoever we can to encourage the return of that. One of the issues and lectures I have given on Zimbabwe over the last 6 years, one of the points I make repeatedly is that a lot of the issues in Zimbabwe arise from historical incidents that have never been resolved, going back, of course, to Gukurahundi in the

1980s when some 20,000 Ndebele were killed over a 2-year period. And I think it was by the fifth brigade, which is trained by the North Koreans. But it even goes beyond that. And a lot of these issues have just been brushed under the rug. People don't like to talk about it.

One of the things I learned from my time in Cambodia in dealing with the Khmer Rouge Tribunal is that, if nothing else, creating a venue where these issues can be brought to light and discussed. Whether they result in judicial punishment or not is actually less important than having them officially and formally acknowledged. So I would definitely argue that the SADC Tribunal, or some similar institution, should be put in place, and it should be a permanent institution to deal with these issues, not just in Zimbabwe, but across the region as a whole. South Africa has issues that are still unresolved that need to be taken care of.

In terms of the issue of sanctions. You have the ZDERA on the one hand, which addresses the country's debt and its international loans. And if I am not mistaken, actually Zimbabwe is not even eligible to apply for loans currently because of its arrears to the international financial institutions. And so leaving ZDERA in place, it is a handy tool to have for later, but it has no impact.

Now, the other issue, the people often get confused between ZDERA and the administrative sanctions, which came in 2 years later. These, I think, are the real immediate stick that we can use. But people have to understand that these sanctions are not against the country in its entirety, but against specific individuals and specific entities. I think a lot of people here in the U.S. misunderstand that.

And it does not limit or prohibit commercial transactions. I am still a firm believer in revitalizing and strengthening the private sector as a counterweight against an out-of-control government. One of the ways that ZANU-PF and the military and security services manage to maintain such control is people have no place else to turn. If you had a stronger private sector, as we have seen in places like Korea, I was in Korea in the 1970s when it was still a dictatorship. Watching the development of a vibrant middle class, and of an economy that was growing and creating jobs, has created a completely different career. It went from a military dictatorship still evolving, but it is now, I think, the 13th largest economy in the world, and growing.

This, I believe, can be done in places like Africa as well. Zimbabwe has the infrastructure. It has an educated population; has an energetic population, when given the opportunity to act. And if the private sector were invigorated and strengthened, I think you could see eventually incrementally, over time, changes in the right direction in the country.

Mr. SMITH. Do we know where Mnangagwa stands on the SADC issue?

Ambassador RAY. Mr. Chairman, I don't think anyone but Mnangagwa knows where he stands on any issue.

Mr. SMITH. But is it something you think we should press with him?

Ambassador RAY. I think we should press with him the return of the SADC Tribunal. As I said in my statement, we should reach out now to this government and lay out our wishes, if you will, or our vision for where things should go. And that, I think, should be one of the things on the list of to-do items.

Mr. SMITH. Okay. I appreciate that.

Would anyone else on the panel want to address any of those questions?

Yes.

Mr. FREETH. Just briefly on the United Nations convention against torture. Zimbabwe is one of the very, very few countries around the world that has not signed that United Nations convention against torture. It is one of the few blank spots on the world map. And so, torture is able to take place in Zimbabwe without that U.N. convention coming into being. So that is something that we need to look at.

Mr. SMITH. Yes.

Ms. DENDERE. I was going to add that while the numbers are the people have been arrested for political engagement unclear. In the new dispensation, as it has been called, they remain quite a few people who are in prison for politically related protests. And the numbers are quite alarming when you look at women. But beyond that, there have been individuals who have been disappeared during the Mugabe regime, and those individuals we have not had any feedback from the government on whether they have been increase. In particular, Itai Dzamara, who disappeared a few years ago, President Mnangagwa at the time was the minister of justice and promised that there was going to be an inquiry and a hearing on where this man went, because his family has not been able to grieve for him to or bury him.

And so such incidents is—it is really important for the government to address that. And if Itai Dzamara is alive, that he should be released; and if, God forbid, he has passed on, then his family deserves to know that as well.

Mr. SMITH. Last week, I chaired a hearing with Marco Rubio on Tibet. We cochair the China Commission. And from a trip there, many trips there in the past from work on China since I got elected to Congress in 1981, China is in a terrible, terrible race to the bottom with North Korea on human rights abuses. Xi Jinping has crushed religion, crushed NGOs that don't really exist, but any semblance of an NGO. And the consolidation of power harkens back to the Cultural Revolution.

We know that General Chiwenga was in Beijing immediately prior the entire unfolding of the Mugabe situation. I wonder if any of you have any insights as to where China was or might have been in orchestrating or giving a wink or a push for his ouster. And in terms of good or bad governance, what is China's influence? We have had hearings on this subcommittee about China's bad governance rule of law model that it promotes. It is certainly not democracy. It is absolutely not human rights-oriented. So if—perhaps, Ambassador, I think you are getting ready to respond.

Ambassador RAY. Well, my experience with China, 4 years serving in China, and 3 years of dealing with my Chinese counterpart in Zimbabwe, first and foremost, what the Chinese look for in countries like Zimbabwe is their version of stability, because they are basically there to get access to resources. I would, and this is a wild guess, say that I don't think that necessarily it is Chinese-engineered or ordered or orchestrated, the change in government. But I would be quite surprised to find out that that was not part of the discussions that Chiwenga had with his counterparts when he was in China, and that the Chinese answer was probably "Keep it simple. Get it done."

Mr. SMITH. Okay.

Yes, Ms. Lewis.

Ms. LEWIS. I think I would agree with Ambassador Ray that while it may not have been an overt push for the coup, that I am sure there was a seeking of approval or assertions that they wouldn't resist the outcome.

I think more broadly, in looking at the Chinese development model, it is much more exploitative looking for resources, but also employment for Chinese workers. Chinese investment tends to not benefit the African economies. And so we should also be very aware and monitor Chinese actions.

Of course, we know that the Chinese have been supporting the Mugabe regime for many years, hosting his birthday parties very lavishly, recipients of elephants being exported, things of that nature. And so it is certainly not a productive relationship in the way that we would like to see for democracy and human rights in Zimbabwe.

Mr. FREETH. Just very briefly on the Chinese.

It was quite interesting when, under President Mugabe, some of their diamond claims were taken away from them in the Marange diamond fields. And I happened to have breakfast with the European Union Ambassador just after that, and I said, Have you had any interaction with the Chinese Ambassador regarding this situation where the diamond claims have been taken away? And he said, Yes. And I asked, Well, what did the Chinese Ambassador have to say? And he said, Well, normally the Chinese Ambassador is inscrutable. But he said, In this case, it was very clear that he was absolutely mad about what had taken place.

So whether that had contributed to Mugabe falling out of favor with the Chinese or not, we don't actually know. But they are about whatever resources they can get out of a country, and I don't—I suspect that that had something to do with it.

Mr. SMITH. Let me just ask. One of the Achilles heels in many elections everywhere is the election commission or electoral commission.

What are the strengths or weakness, or is there an Achilles heel with the ZEC in Zimbabwe, as far as you know? We have raised this in hearing after hearing after hearing. If you don't get that right, if you don't have free and fair going in, people that will ensure that all the ballots are counted, that all the candidates who could be eligible and meet the—you know, a predetermined criteria are put on the ballot without arbitrarily being excised. How would you assess the ZEC?

Secondly, the faith community, we know that on human rights, they had spoken out, whether it be the Catholic Church or the other Christian churches, very boldly on human rights abuses. Your thoughts on that? I know that the Catholic Church is talking about, you know, a sense of forgiveness because they so desperately, I think, want to see a transition to an all-inclusive Zimbabwe, where everyone really feels a part of it. Your thoughts on the faith community and what role they should play.

And, thirdly, we did invite, again, the administration to be here. Ambassador Yamamoto would most likely be the person who would be here to testify. And I think it is valid that they did say that with the trip coming up with Secretary Tillerson, he had to postpone. It is a matter of delay and not a "I won't show up."

So we will have that hearing, but we are in a very tight window, with the anticipation of this election coming up. I am not sure how that gets pulled together in a credible way so fast. And are the election monitors AU, European American, others being invited to participate with, you know, on-the-ground election monitoring in Zimbabwe?

Ms. DENDERE. This is something I can speak to very eloquently, because it is my area of expertise.

So the first thing is that election monitors will come on invitation at the moment the President has indicated that the European Union could likely monitor elections, that it could monitor elections. But I think what is most important is what you have already pointed out, too. What happens with the Zimbabwe Electoral Commission? And this is where the new dispensation could be a problem for ZANU-PF.

ZANU-PF was able to keep Robert Mugabe out because they had the support of Zimbabweans. They had the support of Zimbabweans because Zimbabweans are now primed to protest. In 2016, I was at home, and I attended about five different protests. We got tear-gassed, we were water-canned, and various things happened.

But in the last week, we saw ZEC announce something they have never done before. They announced that we have had at least 5.2 million people register to vote out of the expected 7 million. I think that the number is a little bit lower because we don't have diaspora vote. Of those 5.2 million that have registered to vote, 60 percent are young people under the ages of 40. Now, it is going to be very difficult for ZEC to oversee a stolen election. And I would show us back to the 2008 election.

The 2008 election, Zimbabweans knew that Morgan Tsvangirai had won. The world knew that Morgan Tsvangirai had won because what happened is that Zimbabweans were posting the results of the election as it went on. So it is—for me, it is not so important that we have physical monitors if the government puts up pushback on that. What is really, really important is that we support the civil service, the civil organizations that are working on elections right now.

The young people, in particular, have created over 20 organizations that are training Zimbabweans every single day on the importance of participating in elections. So the numbers that we received yesterday that say 5.2 million people have registered to vote are incredible.

Now, the question is will the election be violent-free? We know that once there is violence, women, in particular, and young men will withdraw from the political process.

Mr. FREETH. Just on not so much ZEC, but on the way that the process takes place and intimidating people, particularly in the rural areas where I absolutely come from. What happens is the military, certainly in the 2008 election, came around in the runoff election after Morgan Tsvangirai was persuaded to have the runoff. What happened was the military came around from ward to ward, to every constituency. And at night, indoctrinated people and used torture and violence against people in a very brutal way so that by—and this is—this comes from China. This is a Maoist sys- tem of intimidation. So the whole ward is brought together in one central point, and everyone then is indoctrinated through the night. Various people are then pointed out as having sympathized in some way with the opposition. And those people are then tor- tured publicly in front of everyone else in the early hours of the morning. Sometimes very brutally, sometimes to death in front of the whole village within the ward.

And then morning comes, and everything is peaceful. But what has happened also within that process is that, certainly, in our area, what was happening was people were divided up into groups of 10. And then each group of 10 had an order to go to the polling booth. And so if you were in the third group of 10, and you were third in your group of 10, you would be the 33rd person to vote at that polling booth. That is how regimented it was in 2008.

So what we need is not observers that are just going to be there. We tried desperately to get the observers to come out from Harare. They refused to come. They said it was too dangerous for them to come out and actually witness these pungwes, as they are called. We cannot have that kind of situation happening again. At the mo- ment what they are doing is saying "remember 2008." It is not hap- pening yet, but we need people to be brave enough from the inter- national community to come and witness this kind of system so that it cannot happen in 2018.

Ms. LEWIS. On the ZEC question. Looking at the historical legacy of the institution, there will be considerable challenges to holding a free, fair, and credible election. But just a few points on where we stand with, at most, 5 months to an election.

The voter registration exercise is continuing to be ongoing, though the blitz has ended. There still remain voter roll challenges, including deduplication auditing the list, things that have not been completed. And the ZEC has not published an operational plan to date for the elections, which would also include things like procure- ment of ballot papers and other very key technical elements of the electoral process.

We also have the challenge of a new chair of the commission and despite some differing feelings about her personally, new leader- ship in any electoral commission so close to an electoral process is always a challenge.

And then, finally, African election commissions usually require significant technical resources and the financial resources to hold free, fair, and credible elections. And last week, the AU did pledge to support that, because with only 5 months left at most, I think it is a real uphill battle for the ZEC to be able to pull off a process that would meet international standards.

Mr. SMITH. Ms. Bass.

Ambassador RAY. The only thing that I would——
Mr. SMITH. Oh.
Ms. BASS. Go ahead.
Ambassador RAY. Well, the only thing that I would add to that, I think having the international observers on the ground is important. But, as I learned in Sierra Leone in the 1990 and 1996 elections there, the real important check on a lot of these issues is having local observers who are on the ground who understand the culture and the language, but also, that they have the freedom and ability to communicate what they see. And this is something that, particularly in Zimbabwe, is important, and that is, people having free access to means of communication, the ability to freely assemble and to get messages out.

One of the things that we did when I was there as Ambassador, we were forced to do because of the hardliners' determination that I would not meet with too many groups of young people, is we started convening electronic meetings, which they found impossible to control or to interdict. This is an issue, I think, that needs to be looked at. Almost every Zimbabwean over the age of 16 has a smartphone with internet access and onboard camera. Mobilizing these people to observe and report, I think, would go a long way to at least discouraging some of the more egregious actions.

Ms. BASS. Thank you, Mr. Chair.

Following up on this, I believe, Ms. Lewis, you mentioned that the civil service organizations that are in—or that might have been Dr. Dendere. But the importance of, instead of having out-of-the-country election observers, having people who are there.

So my question was is IRI on the ground now? And if so, are you doing the training with Zimbabweans? And if not, are you planning to?

Ms. LEWIS. In terms of observations, we have not—I don't believe, any American organizations have been accredited. I know that that is something that the Embassy is engaging on. However, we are conducting programming focused on civic and voter education, mainly through Zimbabwean partners. And, IRI, in general, would say that this kind of partnership with Zimbabweans to have local solutions to local problems is a priority. There are some really fantastic local organizations engaging in civic and voter education on the ground.

I think one of the challenges they face is the very dramatic shift in the political landscape that has happened. And so, there are opportunities that exist that didn't exist a couple of months ago, perhaps you could say. And so, being able to help them mobilize mainly with resources, I think, is something that the U.S. and other international and regional partners need to look at in the months leading up this electoral process to make sure that Zimbabweans are fully aware of their rights and choices on election day.

Ms. BASS. Thank you.

Dr. Dendere, what more do you think is needed in terms of potential support from us?

Ms. DENDERE. I think strengthening the independence media, which I mentioned earlier. Access to information is really critical. For example, with Voice of America, I am often invited to be a panelist. And what I really like is that Voice of America allows

Zimbabweans from very remote areas to call in. We have also seen a lot of participation through what is up on other social media platforms. But the internet is very expensive. But young people have come up with very creative ways to reach wider audiences. So these are things that certainly need to be taken care of.

And I think Mr. Freeth is absolutely right that in rural areas where the fear of violence is very real, a lot of people still remember what happened before independence. They remember the violence of both the Smith regime and even the guerillas that we were fighting for freedom. So I think being able to work with organizations that educate people and their rights, how to report to the police when violence has occurred, and also how to hold the police accountable.

So this is a really good time to work with the police, because the police is kind of on the outs. Their faction lost in the ZANU-PF war, so the government will be quite eager to hold them to account. Ms.

BASS. So what do you think the prospects are for keeping the internet intact during this whole—you know, during the elections, whether or not it would be shut down?

Ms. DENDERE. So——

Ms. BASS. Whether access would be shut—well, you know, that this happened in?

Ms. DENDERE. Yes. In 2016, Pastor Evan Mawarire and others, going back to Chairman Smith's question on religious organizations. Pastor Evan Mawarire and others called us together and called for a shutdown. We woke up in the morning. No one had any plans to leave home.

I went for a run. I came back, and my phone wasn't working. But this is the brilliance of having a country of young people. As I was trying to figure out how to get online, people were wondering, Why aren't you online? And someone sent me a text message that said the internet is not working. They said, Well, do you know what VPN is?

And even as we think about China as a problematic partner, young people in China were actually the ones sending VPN codes to young people in Zimbabwe.

Ms. BASS. Wow. Really?

Ms. DENDERE. So within an hour, we were all back online. We had figured out—I still don't know how to use the VPN, but my 16-year-old niece had put VPN on my phone. The shutdown was going on. And so—and even in my new research, I have been looking at the incidence of shutting down the internet across African countries, if the OPI has learned how to do that.

But I think what also works with Zimbabwe is that the government officials really like being online. One of the first things that President Mnangagwa did when he came into office was to legitimize his Facebook page. So he had a live video. He had a live video and Twitter.

So the way internet works is that they cannot shut it down for the rest of the country and keep it for themselves. So we just hope that their passion for being online will outweigh their needs to restrict our access for the rest of the country.

Ms. BASS. That is very hopeful. That is a very hopeful sign.

Mr. Freeth, did you have something you wanted to add to that?

Mr. FREETH. Not really. I think the big difference between 2008 elections and 2018 is this very thing, that everyone now has got a cell phone. Yes, in 2016, we all had that same experience, and it was incredible how people got around it, and how suddenly we were all able to be online when they are trying to switch us all off. So people make a plan. We are a country of people that make a plan.

Ms. BASS. Well, you mentioned in your opening comments something about a decision that was going to be signed tomorrow, and I didn't know what you were referring to.

Mr. FREETH. That is a decision in South Africa in the high court of South Africa from the judge president and two other judges who— we took a case against President Zuma, along with the law society and various other legal groups which aims to show that President Zuma's actions in signing away—or signing the new pro- tocol to the SADC Tribunal which takes away the individual's rights to go to the SADC Tribunal makes the SADC Tribunal into an interstate court. So if Zambia and Zimbabwe had a dispute over an island in the Zambezi, for example, it could possibly be used for an interstate dispute.

But that wasn't what the original protocol was all about. It wasn't what the SADC Treaty was all about. It is not what SADC, which is there to promote human rights, rule of law, and democracy is all about. And so when President Zuma signed that bit of paper, he did it without the cabinets' approval, without Parliament even looking at it, without a consultation of the people of South Africa.

So we took a case against President Zuma to say that he acted unconstitutionally; that he acted against the SADC Treaty; that he had acted irrationally, in fact. And we are going to get that judgment tomorrow, and we are very hopeful that it will be a good judgment and it will set the tone for other SADC countries to then say, you are right, South Africa. Our President also did the same thing, and it was irrational and unconstitutional against the SADC Treaty.

Ms. BASS. Thank you.

Ambassador Ray, thinking about moving forward in U.S. policy, you know, you made a few comments about the carrot and stick. You talked about actions that I believe we could take to invigorate the economy, but you also specifically said you didn't see lifting sanctions. So I wanted to just ask you about that. I mean, you said, you know, the possibility of it if things got better. But, for example, we have travel sanctions against Mnangagwa. So what if the election is determined to be fair and free, should that be lifted? And then, how do we move our policy forward to help reinvigorate the economy if we also have the economic sanctions? You talked about the Korean example. And if we promoted something like that in Zimbabwe, then how would it be overseen?

So I kind of wanted you to talk about, more specifically, how we would move forward in changing our policy as things develop, hopefully in a positive direction, in Zimbabwe.

Ambassador RAY. Well, I will take the issue of sanctions first.

The administrative sanctions against certain individuals, and Mnangagwa is on that list of individuals, seizes their assets here in the U.S., bank accounts and property, and limits their travel to the U.S., other than for U.N. events. I think——

Ms. BASS. What about coming here to meet with the State Department?

Ambassador RAY. I am sorry?

Ms. BASS. What about—the human events is one thing. But what if he were to come here?

Ambassador RAY. There are—the way it worked when I was there, if a Zimbabwean official was in New York at the U.N., and wanted to meet with someone in the State Department here in Washington, they apply for a special permission to do that. There are—it is a convoluted process, but there are ways to work it.

While I am against a wholesale lifting of all of the sanctions, one of the things I argued vehemently for when I was Ambassador is a more flexible administrative sanctions regime. And I think that is what we should look at in case the election is free and fair, and we have a President Mnangagwa in July or August 2018, to allow a more—an easier process to enable us to engage him to the degree we should to try be able to push him in the direction we want him to go.

And so, there is nothing in the administrative sanctions that says we cannot say—for example, say to a person, You are the President of the country. You can travel to Washington. You can travel to New York. And I think that is probably one way that we can, shall we say, tighten the screw.

I once said to someone when I was asked if I was averse to twisting arms, I said, No, but I have to be able to take the hand first before I can twist the arm. And so I think we need to look at that. And other sanctions, when I talk about reinvigorating, or invigorating, if you will, the private sector, actually, the sanctions regime except for the fact that a couple of Zimbabwe's banks are on the list, shouldn't have an impact on that. There is a certain amount of two-way trade currently existing between our countries, and there are—I think FedEx, or one of the big packaging compa-nies has a presence there. Ford has a presence there. Cargill is there. Coca-Cola is there. And several other American companies have presence in Zimbabwe, have investments in Zimbabwe. They are not that huge.

But I think that if we looked at ways to strengthen the private sector contacts between nonsanctioned economic entities in Zimbabwe, and commercial entities here, you create a stronger middle class, which is a little harder to intimidate and to coerce.

Ms. BASS. Thank you very much—oh, I am sorry.

Go ahead.

Ms. LEWIS. Just to add one thing, in terms of the sanctions, in looking at, perhaps, some relief in that area, it is important that these elections be considered free, fair, and credible. But that is not the end point of, you know, what our conditions should be. Elections are just one point in the democratic process and the reform process. There are many, many other areas of governance and policy in Zimbabwe that need to be looked at to help ensure us that we are on the right path moving forward.

Really, the elections we should be concerned about are the ones after the 2018 elections, when there is a more conducive political

environment to free and fair competition. And so we should keep—
—

Ms. BASS. Well, I agree with you in terms of these elections. As a matter of fact, in my opening comments, I stated that. Specifically, the reason why I asked is because of the President and because he is specifically named.

But having said that, what is our policy moving forward? How do we—I mean, I would like to be hopeful. If it doesn't turn out in a hopeful way, then clearly we can stay with the status quo. But if it does, what is the pathway and what is the best thing for us to do?

Ambassador RAY. I think that is why it is important that we engage, because in order to achieve this, everyone on the Zimbabwean side and on our side has to have a clear understanding of what it is we are asking or demanding, if you will, they do.

Ms. BASS. Exactly.

Ambassador RAY. And so that is why I think our application of the sanctions to individuals needs to be flexible to enable the degree of engagement that can achieve that. We need to sit down with them—well, we need to sit down with ourselves first and decide just what it is we want them to do——

Ms. BASS. Right.

Ambassador RAY [continuing]. So that we don't ask them for more than they are capable of giving but that we don't fall into the trap of accepting from them less than they are capable of giving.

Ms. BASS. Right.

Thank you. Thank you very much.

Mr. SMITH. And on that last point, Mr. Ambassador, that is exactly why we are having this hearing. We wanted to hear from four experts, people who have lived it and are knowledgeable, so that we could hopefully craft a good response. And our next hearing will be with the administration.

Before you go, I do have just two final questions.

If the other three panelists, if you would like to speak to the issue of the faith-based community, the clergy, what role they are playing. You know, in DR Congo, and I have been there, as a matter of fact, Greg Simpkins, who is now at USAID now—Greg, we miss you—we have been to the DR Congo together, and I can tell you that the church plays a major role in elections, not just things of the spirit, humanitarian efforts, human rights advocacy, which they do so superbly well, but also, they do great work in the election area. Is that something that they are being brought in to in Zimbabwe?

And, secondly, Zimbabwe gets a "not free" designation from Freedom House when it comes to press freedoms. Have you seen any amelioration of that stranglehold that Mugabe had on the media of all kinds? Is there maybe an opening, a little bit more independence, the ability of an editor to write an editorial that is more critical without fear, because that would be certainly a very positive trend line?

Anybody want to address this?

Ambassador RAY. I can't really speak too authoritatively to the circumstances after I left in 2012. 2009 to 2012, there was a little modification of the press space. There were a number of independent newspapers, not very super performers but at least they were there. There was at least one, perhaps two, radio stations that were independent.

Where there was an absolute government iron fist was on televised—on television. One TV network in the entire country controlled by the government. So it was a mixed bag. I mean, you had independent print journals that weren't, in my opinion, very professional. You had a state-controlled newspaper. The only thing you could trust were the sports scores. The radio—I think, a lot of Zimbabweans, even in ZANU-PF, got a lot of their credible news from VOA and BBC.

So there is a lot of work to be done there. And, again, I think, this goes to the whole issue of invigorating the private sector, because in order to be effective, the newspapers, the radio, or to set up an independent TV network, it requires money. And if you have a reasonably affluent middle class, you have a private sector that is growing, then you have the source of funds to be able to create these things. A lot of the independent newspapers, for example, were the toys of some wealthy Zimbabwean who had an ax to grind, and that is just not a—that is not a recipe for a very good professional independent press.

Ms. DENDERE. So on the faith-based communities, it is interesting to talk about the faith-based communities and corruption in one hand. So in my statement, I say that the single biggest problem for Zimbabwe is corruption. And how does this relate to the church?

Over the last 5 years, we have seen an increase in evangelical changes that sometimes have 5,000 to 10,000 people showing up. But what we have also seen is that the church has been used as a football, in some ways, between the ZANU-PF factions. So in the last week, we have seen one of the most popular young prophets now being brought in on acts of corruption.

Where I saw some green light was at Morgan Tsvangirai's funeral, where members of the Methodist church spoke very openly and said things that we haven't heard from the church in a long time. They say that since 2009, they were very involved in engaging with Morgan Tsvangirai on the unity government. We also saw Father Korneri (ph) playing an important role during the coup/non coup situation in November.

So I think when the government does not punish people for speaking up, then even the church will be strengthened. But as long as Zimbabwe doesn't address its corruption, then every sector from the church to the media to the banks is in serious trouble, because now you had churches that were being used to funnel funds outside for ZANU-PF people. And then you can't say with certainty whether this church actually represents the interests of the people, or whether the church represents the interest of the individuals.

So corruption is very epidemic, and it now affects every single facet of Zimbabwean life in very problematic ways. And so if we are able to address that, that could be a solution.

And then on the independent media, the media is not free and fair. The Herald still controls the media. I doubt that they would publish that someone like—something that I would write, right?

They wouldn't publish that regardless of how I feel about the government. And I think that is a problem.

At the same time, we also have a lot of print media. But as the Ambassador has said, sometimes the quality is problematic. But I do want to highlight that the U.S. Embassy in Zimbabwe is doing amazing work working with journalists already. And as we transition to the next Ambassador, I hope that those programs will continue to receive funding. Beyond the work that the United States is doing, independent journalists have also been training themselves and being very engaged. But, again everyone I have spoken to is really worried that once this phase has passed, and if the government starts to feel that they are under threat, then maybe this veneer of freedom that we are seeing might be taken away so that—I mean, we are not sure what would happen with that.

Mr. SMITH. Yes.

Mr. FREETH. I think you can be sure that the state media will report us all in the Herald and other more radical newspapers like the Patriot tomorrow or in the coming days. It is a foregone conclusion.

As far as faith-based communities are concerned, the Christian community in Zimbabwe is huge. And there is no politician that can draw people like the churches can draw people. And so there has been a kind of—over the years, there has been—people have lost all kind of faith, as it were, in political transition. And it is the churches that have become the area of focus for people. And so, when Pastor Evan rose up and started for the first time as a church leader speaking out strongly, people just flocked to him. And what happened in July 2016 was one of the most phenomenal things that I have ever been a part of.

In the past, the church has been very afraid. But I think that cloak of fear is being gradually thrown off. And there are church leaders that are starting to stand up for justice issues and starting to talk about justice issues for the first time. And I think this needs to be really encouraged in a major way. I think it is exciting. I think it is very important that the church is able to be the moral voice of the nation, and I think it is starting to happen.

Mr. SMITH. I thank all of you for your tremendous testimony. Hopefully, we can take this and really have an impact in terms of policy, because your insights have been outstanding.

I would just note parenthetically that Greg Simpkins, again, who is here, used to be our chief of staff on the subcommittee, and now Piero, who is our general counsel. In 2015, they were in Zimbabwe and were called American spies by the media. You know, it reminds me, when I was in China on one of my human rights trips, Wei Jingsheng, the father of the democracy world movement, who spent about 20 years in the gulag, the loud guys they call it there, tortured horribly in China. When I met with him when he was let out briefly before getting rearrested, they interrogated him and said I was a CIA spy. One big lie. I mean, I am a Member of Congress. They're top staffers who have a huge impact. We do have a CIA, but we are not part of it. But it is amazing how they think that somehow it is a slur. And it is just like a boomerang that says what kind of media are you that would do that?

Without objection, we have a number of testimonies for the record. This is from Craig Richardson, Dr. Richardson, and also the timeline of Mike Campbell, which has been provided, of course, in the Campbell case. Without objection, these will be made a part of the record. And if our distinguished witnesses would like to add anything to the record, please do. Just send it to us, and we will include it, because we want it to be as thorough as possible.

Thank you so very much. The hearing is adjourned.

[Whereupon, at 3:45 p.m., the subcommittee was adjourned.]

APPENDIX

Material Submitted for the Record

SUBCOMMITTEE HEARING NOTICE
COMMITTEE ON FOREIGN AFFAIRS
U.S. HOUSE OF REPRESENTATIVES
WASHINGTON, DC 20515-6128

Subcommittee on Africa, Global Health, Global Human Rights, and International Organizations
Christopher H. Smith (R-NJ), Chairman

February 21, 2018

TO: MEMBERS OF THE COMMITTEE ON FOREIGN AFFAIRS

You are respectfully requested to attend an OPEN hearing of the Committee on Foreign Affairs to be held by the Subcommittee on Africa, Global Health, Global Human Rights, and International Organizations in Room 2172 of the Rayburn House Office Building (and available live on the Committee website at http://www.ForeignAffairs.house.gov):

DATE: Wednesday, February 28, 2018

TIME: 2:00 p.m.

SUBJECT: Zimbabwe After Mugabe

WITNESSES: The Honorable Charles A. Ray
                   (*Former U.S. Ambassador to Zimbabwe*)

                   Ms. Elizabeth Lewis
                   Regional Deputy Director
                   Africa Division
                   International Republican Institute

                   Mr. Ben Freeth
                   Executive Director
                   Mike Campbell Foundation

                   Chipo Dendere, Ph.D.
                   Visiting Assistant Professor
                   Amherst College

By Direction of the Chairman

COMMITTEE ON FOREIGN AFFAIRS

MINUTES OF SUBCOMMITTEE ON _Africa, Global Health, Global Human Rights, and International Organizations_ HEARING

Day __Wednesday__ Date ____2/28/18____ Room ____2172____

Starting Time __2:01pm__ Ending Time __3:45pm__

Recesses |____| (____to____) (____to____) (____to____) (____to____) (____to____) (____to____)

Presiding Member(s)

Chairman Smith

Check all of the following that apply:

Open Session ☑
Executive (closed) Session ☐
Televised ☐

Electronically Recorded (taped) ☐
Stenographic Record ☑

TITLE OF HEARING:

Zimbabwe After Mugabe

SUBCOMMITTEE MEMBERS PRESENT:

Ranking Member Bass

NON-SUBCOMMITTEE MEMBERS PRESENT: _(Mark with an * if they are not members of full committee.)_

Chairman Royce

HEARING WITNESSES: Same as meeting notice attached? Yes ☑ No ☐
(If "no", please list below and include title, agency, department, or organization.)

STATEMENTS FOR THE RECORD: _(List any statements submitted for the record.)_

-Smith: Congressional Statement on the Importance of Property Rights in Zimbabwe, by Craig J.
Richardson, Ph.D.

-Smith: The Campbell Case Timeline

TIME SCHEDULED TO RECONVENE __________
or
TIME ADJOURNED ______________

Subcommittee Staff Associate

MATERIAL SUBMITTED FOR THE RECORD BY THE HONORABLE CHRISTOPHER H. SMITH, A REPRESENTATIVE IN CONGRESS FROM THE STATE OF NEW JERSEY, AND CHAIRMAN, SUBCOMMITTEE ON AFRICA, GLOBAL HEALTH, GLOBAL HUMAN RIGHTS, AND INTERNATIONAL ORGANIZATIONS

February 24, 2018

Congressional Statement on the Importance of Property Rights in Zimbabwe

By Craig J. Richardson, Ph.D.

BB&T Distinguished Professor of Economics
Department of Economics and Finance
Winston-Salem State University, North Carolina

Author: The *Collapse of Zimbabwe in the Wake of the 2000-2003 Land Reforms*, (Mellen Press, 2004) and numerous other articles on Zimbabwe. Examples include op-eds on Zimbabwe in *The Wall Street Journal* (most recently, January 24, 2018) and many peer-reviewed academic journals. This statement draws from Prof. Richardson's 15+ years of extensive research into Zimbabwe's economy.

Introduction: The impact of the 2000-2017 Zimbabwean land reforms on its economy

For the past 17 years, Zimbabwe has become "Exhibit A" on how to wreck a national economy. In the early 2000s, the Mugabe-led government seized thousands of large-scale commercial farms without compensating the landholders who held the property titles. Farms were often given to political cronies who knew little about farming or broken into hundreds of smaller plots for subsistence farming. As a result, private agricultural property became nationalized and incentives to manage and develop the land dropped sharply. Property titles for the farms became worthless, and banks holding the deeds went out of business or reduced credit availability, because mortgage payments were no longer being made. Hundreds of retail and commercial businesses dependent upon the farming sector also failed, and government tax revenue rapidly shrank as a result, creating enormous budget deficits in the mid 2000s.

Cascading effects of broken property rights

The land seizures symbolized an overall breakdown in rule of law. Foreign investors fled and spooked tourists changed travel plans, creating even more of a downward economic spiral. The country formerly known as the breadbasket of Africa (which had exported its agricultural surplus) was now dependent upon food aid from the outside world, as the new farmers often had little knowledge of farming. To make matters worse, the farms' assets, such as its tractors, buildings, and irrigation equipment, were often stripped and sold by the new owners, who pocketed the cash.

By 2005, the loss of the country's wealth from the land seizures alone—at $5.3 billion—was calculated to be more than all the foreign aid Zimbabwe had received since its independence in 1980.

The government filled the gap by printing money. According to the OECD, the acute food shortages caused by the land reforms meant that the country, which was once a net exporter of maize, had to print billions of Zimbabwean dollars to import food. The government even ran out of hard currency to buy the imported ink needed to manufacture its own money; as a result, bills were only printed on one side. By March 2006, it took Z$60,000 to buy one loaf of bread, even as a new Z$50,000 note was being printed to "keep up" with the demands of higher prices. The hyperinflation increased each month at an exponential rate. Johns Hopkins University economist Steve Hanke calculated that, by November 2008, Zimbabwe's annual inflation was the second highest in history, at 79.6 sextillion percent. To put that in perspective, Hanke calculated that prices were doubling every 24.7 hours. After dollarization in early January 2009, inflation immediately fell to −2.3 percent by the end of the month and stabilized thereafter.

<u>Dollarization in 2009: Stopping the freefall, but not fixing the true problem</u>

Since dollarization stabilized the economy, Zimbabwe could now collect taxes far more efficiently than it could with hyperinflation, which had made accounting nearly impossible for anyone in business or government. By comparison, at the end of 2008 only a paltry $133 million in taxes was collected, but by 2011 tax revenue had jumped to $2.6 billion, according to the IMF. There were pressing needs for infrastructure improvements in roads, bridges, schools, and hospitals, and government wages needed adjustment because of the previous decade's hyperinflation. But despite the more than 1,800 percent rise in tax collections over those three years, government expenditures rose even faster. As a result, deficits climbed from $124 million in 2008 to $583 million in 2011.

Thus, dollarization failed to discipline the government's deficit spending. One reason for this failure is that the IMF and the Chinese government have given Zimbabwe hundreds of millions of dollars in grants and loans since 2009. As a result of the worldwide financial crisis, the IMF gave the Zimbabwean government a one-time $500 million hardship grant in 2008, issued in special drawing rights (SDRs), and encouraged Zimbabwe to spend the money internally on projects such as power stations, railways, and agricultural inputs. Yet in searching for ways to pay for its deficit spending, the Zimbabwean government is finding it increasingly difficult to borrow from the outside world. The government has been in default on most of its external debt, which in 2011 was estimated to be around 10 billion U.S. dollars, or 108 percent of Zimbabwe's nominal GDP. Thus, these grants effectively forestalled real and significant economic reforms.

Given its status of default, Zimbabwe is not currently eligible for new loans from the World Bank or the IMF. This debt stems primarily from loans made in the 1980s and 1990s by private lenders such as banks; foreign governments, including France, Germany, and the United Kingdom; and multilateral institutions including the World Bank, African Development Bank, and (until recently) the IMF. By 2009, the largest multilateral creditor was the World Bank ($1.3 billion in loans outstanding), followed by the African Development Bank ($660 million in loans outstanding).

Gideon Gono, Zimbabwe's Federal Reserve governor, noted in a 2012 government report that its default status in the Western world prevents Zimbabwe from taking on even more debt, saying, "The continued accumulation of external payment arrears has seriously undermined the country's creditworthiness, and severely compromised the country's ability to secure new financing from both bilateral and multilateral sources."

Unlike richer countries, which can sell bonds to attempt to restructure their debt, Zimbabwe only has its natural and physical assets left. But even if Zimbabwe sold all of its mineral rights to the future receipts of diamonds, gold, and platinum, the IMF estimates the present discounted value still wouldn't be enough to pay off all it owes.

Meanwhile, Zimbabwe's true wealth- land's ability to transform equity into economic development by serving as collateral for loans- is locked up. Billions of dollars of this "dead capital", far exceeding the potential receipts of its natural resources, are inaccessible due to property being nationalized instead of privately owned.

<u>Property rights- the foundation of all economic development and builder of trust</u>

The main problem of Zimbabwe's economic collapse is directly tied to the government's severe weakening of property rights, particularly in its agricultural sector. Without these rights, a person without a land title has little ambition to plan and invest over the long term. Titles in farmland lead to long-term investment in capital equipment as well as soil and water management. Thus, they vastly increase agricultural activity; more importantly, they diversify the economy as described earlier and shield it from commodity price shocks. An analogy is a retirement fund that has investment in one stock versus a broad portfolio. The healthiest economies in the world exhibit this diversification, leading to more stable growth, making it a far easier place to plan for one's future.

The current system of nationalized land constrains poor Zimbabwean farmers to a life that will likely never get much better. It makes the country ever more dependent on the help of hundreds of millions of dollars in outside aid each year. Even worse, a person without a land title has little ambition to plan and invest over the long term, since there is no way to capture the accrued value in the land by selling it. This creates an ongoing "need" for aid agencies to provide food, dams, training, and the like, instead of the economy generating a self-sustaining system. When all the aid is added together, it is enormous in scale—jumping from $350 million in 2009 to an estimated $770 million in 2011. This was equal to 30 percent of all government spending in 2011, and 8.6 percent of GDP.

A lack of property rights also heightens Zimbabwe's vulnerabilities to changes by donor countries in their international priorities. In 2018, The Trump administration says it is threatening to substantially cut aid to Zimbabwe. For example, the USAID program that addresses climate change-induced drought in Zimbabwe was launched by the U.S. government in 2013, with $175 million in long- and short-term funding is in jeopardy. Today, USAID-funded projects aimed at curbing the worst effects of climate change can be found across Zimbabwe, and those projects are currently benefiting more than a million people in food insecure rural areas. That could easily change according to the whims of one administration.

Recent changes since Mugabe's departure- are 99 year leases enough?
Since Mugabe's departure last year, there have been some positive moves towards reversing some of the damaging land reform policies, by the government halting the ongoing seizures. President Mnangagwa announced the formation of 99-year leases for government-owned farmland, which are a large improvement over previous leases of just 5 years. However, this arrangement will ultimately limit the recovery of Zimbabwe and trust by the outside world in terms of foreign direct investment.

For example, these leases still create much uncertainty both within Zimbabwe and beyond. Will domestic banks accept these leases as collateral? If so, will the land be able to be transferred to banks, and then sold by auction to other individuals? Will foreigners buy this land if they have the same concerns? Can these leases be sold and transferred to other individuals?

The answers to the above questions are a likely "no." What is clear is that all of this uncertainty lowers the value of the land and thus the potential for the country to rebound.

Freehold land titles involve a much simpler transfer of deeds between institutions and owners. They communicate effectively to the rest of the world in a language all developed countries understand, that private property rights are the key to economic development and progress. These types of property rights ultimately improve a country's economic complexity due to the rich variety of enterprises that spring from bank financing and collateral. For example, a farmer who uses his land to buy a tractor creates a demand beyond just the farming equipment. New auxiliary enterprises spring up, including retail enterprises selling spare parts (tires, engine parts), specialized labor (mechanics, tractor drivers), new types of seeds, irrigation equipment, and more. Farmers also invest in dams and reservoirs, enabling them to mitigate the damaging consequences of droughts and climate change. By enabling a sharp increase in labor productivity, the tractor creates a wide variety of jobs and businesses that are far more stable than subsistence farming. These are some of the subtle benefits of property rights often hidden from view and unmeasured. Without freehold property titles, wealth is locked up and only the meager income from the land itself can be obtained.

Concluding thoughts and observations: Mitigating the costs of social change
It would be naïve to suggest that a quick moving of land ownership from 99-year leases and communal ownership will proceed without problems. Any change has its costs. Local village chiefs often (but not always) oppose moves to freehold titles because they no longer can exercise control over who owns what land and for how long. The cultural and social status of the chief

becomes diminished with the introduction of private property, unless the chief is persuaded of the benefits to both him and his people in the long run. Villagers may also like the stability of knowing who their neighbors will be, without fully appreciating how communal property rights can also trap them in subsistence living. Care thus must be taken to appreciate these cultural factors, using models of villages that have allow visitors to see how property rights transform people's standard of living. Villagers can see how a rich variety of choices improve chances for better jobs and career paths for their children, along with better health outcomes. If chiefs can take on new roles in the village, or given some form of compensation, the road to property rights may enjoy a smoother path that allows all Zimbabweans to rise to a higher level of economic development. Foreign investors are waiting in the wings for this to happen. When it does, Zimbabwe will eventually return to being the "bread-basket" of Africa, with little to no need for ongoing foreign aid.

MATERIAL SUBMITTED FOR THE RECORD BY THE HONORABLE CHRISTOPHER H. SMITH, A REPRESENTATIVE IN CONGRESS FROM THE STATE OF NEW JERSEY, AND CHAIRMAN, SUBCOMMITTEE ON AFRICA, GLOBAL HEALTH, GLOBAL HUMAN RIGHTS, AND INTERNATIONAL ORGANIZATIONS

23 February 2018

THE CAMPBELL CASE: ZIMBABWEAN LANDMARK FARM TEST CASE

TIME LINE

Mike Campbell (Pvt) Ltd v Zimbabwe

Mike Campbell (Pvt) Ltd et al. v. Republic of Zimbabwe is a case decided by the Southern African Development Community (SADC) Tribunal in Windhoek, Namibia. The Tribunal held that the Zimbabwean Government violated the organisation's treaty by denying access to the courts and engaging in racial discrimination against white farmers whose lands had been confiscated under the land reform program in Zimbabwe.

This is the time line of the case of William Michael Campbell of Mount Carmel farm and 77 additional commercial farmers whose case was joined to the Campbell case:

- ❑ **1999:** Mike Campbell [Private Limited] purchased Mount Carmel farm in the Chegutu district of Zimbabwe legally in 1999. (Every farm bought after 1980 had to be offered to the Government first for land redistribution and then deeds were stamped "No Government Interest" if they did not wish to purchase it.)

- ❑ **February 2000:** The Government-orchestrated land invasions began in February 2000, immediately after President Mugabe, who had become increasingly unpopular, lost a referendum to further entrench his presidential powers. Although Mugabe claimed this was a land reform programme designed to hand white-owned farmland to poor, landless black Zimbabweans, the primary beneficiaries have been the ruling ZANU-PF elite, notably Politburo members and their family members, security force officers, compliant judges and even church leaders. Initially, so-called "war veterans" were ferried onto farms, often in Government vehicles, displacing their owners and farm workers, leaving thousands homeless and destitute. Their tactics of intimidation, which included theft, violence on an appallingly brutal scale, murder and arson, caused a total breakdown of law and order across the country.

- ❑ **July 2001:** Amid large-scale land invasions by "war veterans", Campbell received a Government notice to acquire Mount Carmel farm, but the notice was declared invalid by the High Court.

- ❑ **2003:** Most commercial farmers had been displaced and more than 200,000 farm workers and their families – an estimated one million people – had lost their jobs and homes, as well as their access to farm schools, farm clinics and other social amenities. This was despite the fact that the Government's own land audit showed that 2.8 million ha of farmland lay idle.

- ❑ **January 2004:** The Land Acquisition Amendment Act was passed. This enables the Mugabe Government to block any legal action against it taking farms away from their owners. Once the farmer has been issued with this "legal" document, he is confined to his house and forbidden from doing anything on his land, even if he has a crop that needs to be harvested. Not abiding by these restrictions could mean two years imprisonment. The farmer can remain in his house for three more months, after which, he has to get out. There is no compensation.

❑ **July 2004:** A new notice of intent to acquire Mount Carmel was published in the official Government Gazette, but no acquisition notice was actually issued. However, two months later, according to court filings, "persons purported to occupy the farm on behalf of ZANU PF spokesman Nathan Shamuyarira, claiming the former minister had been allocated the farm." After three more preliminary notices to take the farm were published in 2004, Campbell applied to the High Court for a protection order.

Note: The Government of Zimbabwe had been attempting to seize Mount Carmel since July 2001 but these were at first thwarted by the High Court of Zimbabwe.

❑ **14 September 2005:** The Constitution of Zimbabwe Amendment (No. 17) Act of 2005 came into effect. Amendment 17 transferred title of all land previously "acquired" for resettlement purposes to the State. It prohibited court challenges to the acquisitions and allowed the Government to acquire any land that had been agricultural land in the last 50 years by simply publishing a notice of acquisition in the newspaper.

❑ **15 May 2006:** Lawyers for Mike Campbell launched proceedings in the Supreme Court of Zimbabwe challenging the constitutional validity of Amendment 17. This served to delay the eviction of the applicant, but it became clear that no permanent protection would be found within the Zimbabwe legal system since the court heard the constitutional challenge but reserved judgment for 6 months.

❑ **December 2006:** The Gazetted Land (Consequential Provisions) Act passed into law, requiring all farmers whose land was compulsorily acquired by the Government - and who were not in possession of an official offer letter, permit, or lease, to cease to occupy, hold, or use that land within 45 days and to vacate their homes within 90 days. Failure to comply is a criminal offence punishable by a fine and a maximum prison sentence of up to two years. Only a small number of farmers received an offer letter or lease. Although 800 commercial farmers subsequently applied for Government authority to remain on their farms, none was granted. (Dale Dore)

❑ **October 2007:** 11 white commercial farmers, including Mike Campbell, appeared before the Chegutu magistrate's court accused of failing to leave their gazetted farms. Their appeal against the conviction was rejected. The Zimbabwe Government started prosecuting Campbell for the unique offence of farming his own land - which he had developed into a thriving agricultural enterprise - and living in his own home on the farm.

❑ **5 October 2007:** As the Supreme Court had not responded to enquiries about the challenge to Amendment 17 mounted in May 2006, it was assumed that it had declined to exercise its jurisdiction. Mike Campbell therefore sought relief from the SADC Tribunal in Windhoek, Namibia. (Dale Dore)

[Note: The Tribunal was set up to ensure that SADC member states, including Zimbabwe, adhere to the SADC Treaty and Protocols, protect the rights of citizens, and ensure the rule of law. The scope of the jurisdiction of the SADC Tribunal, as stated in Article 15 (1) of the SADC Protocol, is to adjudicate upon *"disputes between States, and between natural and legal persons and States"*. In terms of Article 15 (2), no person may bring an action against a State without first exhausting all available remedies, or unless the person is unable to proceed under the domestic jurisdiction of such State.]

- **11 October 2007:** Mike Campbell filed a case with the Tribunal challenging the acquisition of Mount Carmel farm. His application contended that the land acquisition process was unlawful under international customary law, the SADC Treaty and the African Charter on Human and People's Rights. Since the case was filed after the Supreme Court in Zimbabwe failed to issue a judgment on the challenge to Amendment 17, Campbell's application was deemed to be within the base and scope of the jurisdiction of the Tribunal. (Dale Dore)

  Campbell's application sought an order from the Tribunal declaring, **first**, that Constitutional Amendment No. 17 violated his fundamental rights protected under Article 6 of the SADC Treaty and, **second**, requesting an interdict to stop the Zimbabwean Government from acquiring his farm.

- The Tribunal concluded that it had jurisdiction to hear the case because the dispute concerned "human rights, democracy and the rule of law", which are binding principles for members of the SADC.

- This landmark case, which was supposed to start on the 20 November 2007, marked the first case to be heard by the SADC Tribunal. Unfortunately the case was delayed since the fax machine in the office of President Mugabe was reportedly broken and the number to which the notice had been sent could not be verified.

  The case was postponed to 4 December 2007, after which it was postponed again to 11 December 2007.

- **11 December 2007:** In reserving judgment after the hearing, the Tribunal issued an interim protection order which stipulated that the Zimbabwe Government should "take no steps - or permit no steps to be taken, directly or indirectly, whether by its agents or by orders, to evict from or interfere with the 'peaceful residence' on and beneficial use of the farms occupied by the farmers, their employees and the families of the employees." Government representatives assured the Tribunal it would abide by the decision.

  This interim relief order was repeated for the other interveners on 28 March 2008.

- **13 December 2007:** The SADC Tribunal, in its first decision since becoming functional in April 2007, ruled in favour of Campbell.

- **22 January 2008:** The Supreme Court of Zimbabwe finally delivered its judgment in the 15 May 2006 case (Campbell and other white farmers). The effect was to dismiss the applicants' entire challenge. Contrary to the accepted norms of natural justice and international law, it ruled that Parliament had the right to oust the jurisdiction of the courts to prevent judicial arbitrations between citizens and the State. The court also refused to countenance the charge that Amendment 17 discriminated against the applicants on the basis of race or colour. (Dale Dore)

  This served to confirm the applicants' prior contention that all legal remedies within Zimbabwe had been exhausted. The only objection to the jurisdiction of the SADC Tribunal advanced by the Government of Zimbabwe was a failure on the part of the applicants to exhaust domestic remedies.

- **End January 2008**: Additional white commercial farmers who were still occupying their farms applied to be joined as interveners in Campbell's pending application before the Tribunal.

  The Tribunal ordered the applications to be heard in March 2008 because the Zimbabwe Government said it required more time to consider and respond to the intervener applications.

- **25 March 2008**: The final hearing of the main action in the SADC Tribunal case was scheduled to commence but was postponed to 28 March.

- **28 March 2008**: Following the hearing, a total of 77 additional commercial farmers were granted leave to intervene. Interim relief similar to that given to Mike Campbell on 13 December 2007 was granted to 74 farmers since three were no longer residing on their farms.

- **7 May 2008**: In a letter to the Registrar of the Tribunal dated 7 May 2008, Zimbabwe's Deputy Attorney–General indicated that he would not be ready to proceed on 28 May 2008 and requested a postponement.

- **27 May 2008**: The legal representatives received information that a group of black resettled Zimbabweans intended to apply to intervene in the court proceedings.

- **28 May 2008**: The Tribunal convened and had to first deal with the application for further intervention on the behalf of the black resettled farmers. Approximately 300 farmers wished to intervene but the supporting documents were not in order.

  The lawyer representing the black farmers admitted to having been approached at short notice and had therefore not had enough time to obtain all the necessary documentation. This was seen as a deliberate delaying strategy and after a brief adjournment the Tribunal ruled that the application for intervention was not in order, thereby refusing it.

  An oral application for postponement of the main case by the Zimbabwe Government was then moved. This was on the basis that the Government had insufficient resources, particularly manpower, to complete the papers on time and, particularly, to gain access to the Applicants' authorities. The Tribunal granted a postponement, directing the Government to file all its papers by 18 June 2008. The hearing was postponed to 16, 17 and 18 July 2008.

- **29 June 2008**: Mike Campbell, his wife Angela and their son-in-law, Ben Freeth, who also lived on and farmed Mount Carmel farm, were abducted and brutally assaulted for nine hours late into the night by "war veterans" and Government militia. After being forced at gunpoint to sign a paper stating that they would withdraw from the SADC Tribunal case, they were driven to the small town of Kadoma, where they were abandoned, but managed to seek help. They were rushed to hospital for emergency medical treatment.

- **16 July 2008:** The case of Mike Campbell and the 77 farmers was heard in Windhoek.

- **17 July 2008: The first contempt application:** Filed a month previously, the first contempt application was also heard. The Zimbabwe Government attempted to block

the application on the grounds that they wanted further time to file papers. This
request was refused because their explanation for the delay was deemed to be feeble.
The Government's legal team was given 30 minutes to take instructions and to present
their argument because they had already had more than 30 days to respond.

When they came back, they indicated to the Tribunal that they were not prepared to
proceed and staged a walkout of the Tribunal led by the Zimbabwean ambassadress to
Namibia, who was sitting with the legal team.

❑ **18 July 2008:** The Tribunal ruled that the applicants had presented "abundant material"
to show the existence of the failure on the part of the respondent (the Zimbabwe
Government) and its agents to comply with the interim relief order of the Tribunal.

❑ **11 September 2008:** The Tribunal reserved judgement on the application. Tribunal
Registrar David Mkandawire said the court was adjourned for judgement to study
objections from the Zimbabwe Government lawyers.

❑ **28 November 2008:** The Tribunal's decision on this date addressed four main issues:

(1) Whether the Tribunal had jurisdiction to hear the case;
(2) Whether the plaintiffs had been denied access to domestic courts in violation of the
SADC Treaty;
(3) Whether the Zimbabwean Government had discriminated against the plaintiffs on
the basis of race, and
(4) Whether the plaintiffs were entitled to compensation.

Decision:

(1) The Tribunal held that it had jurisdiction to hear the case, because Amendment 17
had eliminated the plaintiffs' access to the domestic courts, and the plaintiffs were
therefore entitled to seek remedy before the Tribunal.
(2) The Tribunal found that the plaintiffs had been deprived of their right to a fair
hearing before being deprived of their rights.
(3) On the racial discrimination issue, the Tribunal held that the actions of the
Zimbabwean Government constituted indirect or "de facto" discrimination because
implementation of Amendment 17 affected white farmers only.
(4) Finally, the Tribunal held that the plaintiffs were entitled to compensation for the
expropriation of their lands.

The Tribunal announced in its judgement that "by unanimity the Respondent [the
Zimbabwe Government] is directed to take all necessary measures through its agents to
protect the possession, occupation and ownership of the lands of the Applicants."

❑ The three exceptions were commercial farmer Christopher Jarrett [Luchabi Ranch,
Nyamandlovu], and agricultural companies Tengwe Estates (Pvt) Ltd [Andrew Kockott,
Urungwe] and France Farm (Pvt) Ltd [Lawrence Cumming, Victoria Falls] who had
already been evicted from their lands. The Zimbabwe Government was directed to pay
them fair compensation, on or before 30 June 2009.

Note: The amount of compensation was not laid down by the court and the applicants
were required to submit comprehensive details of what fair compensation would entail.

Since this would be a critical test case that would determine the compensation parameters for the more than 4,000 dispossessed Zimbabwean farmers, it was vital for the Zimbabwean government that the compensation case should not be heard by the SADC Tribunal.

Immediately after the Judgement, the State-owned Herald newspaper reported that the then Minister of State for National Security, Lands, Land Reform and Resettlement in the President's Office, Didymus Mutasa, had responded that the Tribunal was "daydreaming."

- **23 December 2008:** Mike Campbell made an urgent application to register the judgement in the High Court of Zimbabwe. The urgency of the application was not accepted but no reasons were ever given. Thereafter, a number of other applications were made to have a hearing to register the judgement but none of them were heard either. Meanwhile approximately two hundred additional white farmers were prosecuted for remaining on their farms, despite the SADC Tribunal judgement.

- **January 2009:** The Deputy Chief Justice from the Supreme Court of Zimbabwe rubbished the SADC Tribunal Judgement by saying "it is clear that the Tribunal lacked jurisdiction." Prince Machaya, the deputy Attorney General, also wrote stating that it was Government's position to continue the prosecution of farmers, despite the SADC Tribunal judgement.

- **February 2009 and March 2009:** Mike Campbell faced a number of threatening invasion situations on his farm.

- **March 2009:** The Zimbabwe High Court nullified the SADC Tribunal ruling which said white farmers whose farms were acquired by Government for resettlement purposes could remain on the farms because they had legal title to the farms. The court claimed the SADC Tribunal's decisions did not apply and could not be enforced in Zimbabwe unless Parliament ratified the Protocol that set up the Tribunal.

- **3 April 2009:** Mike Campbell's home was invaded by a gang led by Lovemore Madangonda (known as "Landmine") who worked for ZANU PF heavy weight Nathan Shamuyarira, a former minister and retired Information Secretary. Over the next few days various workers were badly beaten by the invaders – one of them sustaining a fractured skull. Mike Campbell and his wife were eventually forced out of their fully furnished house on 5 April 2009 and were unable to return as the invaders based themselves there.

- **9 April 2009:** All 150 farm workers were forced to stop working and the invaders took the guards' weapons and threatened them with death. The 50 tons of export mangoes in the pack-shed were left to rot. Invaders broke into the shed and took Mike Campbell's tractors to reap the rest of the crops for themselves. Hundreds of thousands of US dollars of crops were stolen.

- **17 April 2009:** Deputy Prime Minister Arthur Mutambara, along with both Ministers of Home Affairs in the coalition Government, the Minister of State in the Prime Minister's Office and the Minister of Lands, visited Mount Carmel farm. They said that Campbell's workers could continue to work and that he could live in his house and reap the remainder of his crops. They stipulated that the invaders must abide by any High Court

Orders that might come out. That afternoon, in defiance of the Ministers, the farm workers who assembled to try to resume farming activities were all chased away again by the invaders and were not allowed to work.

- **20 April 2009:** The Zimbabwean High Court gave a provisional order evicting the invaders. This was served on them the next day, but the situation became very hostile as almost all the invaders were armed with guns. The police consistently failed to give assistance to the deputy sheriff to evict the invaders as per the High Court Order over the next 6 months while the invaders reaped Campbell's crops.

- **27 April 2009:** Armed invaders chased Ben Freeth's workers away on the other side of Mount Carmel farm. Freeth subsequently received death threats from the invaders.

- **30 April 2009:** Another provisional order was gained in the High Court reinforcing the first, but still nothing was done by the police to ensure that it was enforced.

- **5 May 2009:** In response to the second High Court Order being served on the invaders, Ben and Laura Freeth's garden and driveway were ploughed up in the night inside the fence right outside their house by "Landmine" and his invaders. There were threats to burn down their house and burning sacks were lit under the thatched roof. Peter Asani, one of Campbell's foremen, was abducted from his house by the invaders who beat his feet so badly that he was on crutches, with a cast on one of his feet, until July. All the workers then had their electricity and water cut off by the invaders in an effort to force them to move off the farm.

- **7 May 2009:** The invaders surrounded the Freeths' house with armed men and guns were pointed through the windows. The invaders chased away the 40 linen workers on Laura's linen project. Spanish journalists were in the house at the time and the Freeths were concerned for their safety. The invaders eventually left but returned the next day, again with guns, to chase the workers away. They were unable to work for some weeks.

- **14 May 2009:** "Landmine" arrived at the Freeths' house and threatened "bloodshed" while waving a handgun at the back door and pointing it at a guest.

- **25 May 2009 (Africa Day):** The invaders lit a substantial fire in the Freeths' garden and, with threats and further efforts to intimidate the family – which included making a great deal of noise - tried to get them out of their house. The next night approximately 15 of the invaders broke into the thatched homestead and brought burning tyres through the front door and into the courtyard. The Freeths young children (aged 4, 7 and 9) were threatened and one of the invaders shouted that they would eat them. Another invader made frightening hyena noises. When the invaders finally left, they circled the house, whooping like hyenas.

On other SADC Tribunal-protected farms similar state-sanctioned invasions were also taking place with total impunity. No move was made by the Zimbabwe Government to compensate those farmers who were off their farms, despite the Tribunal's order to do so.

- **5 June 2009: The second contempt application:** The SADC Tribunal heard a second contempt application against the Zimbabwe Government where Campbell and another applicant, Richard Thomas Etheredge, filed a new application to declare the Government of Zimbabwe in contempt of court. Their objective was to persuade SADC to take action regarding the Zimbabwe Government's failure to uphold the SADC Treaty - and to enforce the Tribunal's judgement of 28 November 2008.

❑ Despite the SADC Tribunal judgments, "Landmine" continued to use the tractors he had stolen from Campbell to steal the entire maize, sunflower and orange crops without Campbell, the rightful owner of those crops, being able to reap a single maize cob, sunflower head or orange. This theft was reported to police on various occasions during the ensuing weeks and months but the police did nothing to stop it.

❑ **March, April, November 2009:** Various letters were hand-delivered to Morgan Tsvangirai, Prime Minister in the coalition Government, regarding the breakdown in the rule of law and the contempt, and an investigation into this was requested. However, no replies were received.

❑ **20 August 2009:** The SADC Tribunal issued a costs award (or "taxation award" as it is known in legal terminology) in favour of the farmers (the complainants) in the Campbell contempt case of 5 June 2009. In total, the bill was taxed at US$5,816.47 or R112,780. No payment was forthcoming from the Zimbabwe Government.

❑ **30 August 2009:** Four worker families were made homeless, as well as the Freeths, when their houses were burnt down. The home industry factory that employed 40 women was also burnt down. Although arson could not be proved, the fire was lit in the south from which a strong wind was blowing and being a Sunday, the arsonists would have known that the workers were not there to fight it. The invaders were busy driving around with a stolen 2,000 litre spray tank on a stolen tractor that day and would not come to assist. If the Campbells and Freeths had been able to use their own equipment, they would have been able to put out the fire before it burnt down the houses and factory. The Freeths and their workers lost almost everything they possessed.

❑ **31 August 2009:** 10 tons of fertiliser and other items were stolen by the invaders on Mount Carmel but the police did not arrest any of them.

❑ **2 September 2009:** Mike and Angela Campbell's house was also burnt down, along with almost all of its contents.

❑ **8 September 2009:** A bomb was exploded by the army and the police near to the Campbell's house. This was presumably to intimidate the Campbells and Freeths and prevent them from returning to the house. When Ben Freeth went to the house some days later to conduct a loss assessment, he was arrested by two policemen who said that he was not allowed there. One was bare-chested and carried an FN assault rifle. Freeth was taken to the police station along with a news crew that was with him. He challenged the police, explaining that he had every right to be there as there were High Court Orders and a SADC Tribunal judgment that allowed him and his family to farm and live there. The police explained that the law under which he was being taken away was "private and confidential". He was eventually released later that day.

❑ **2 September 2009:** The Zimbabwe Government announced its decision to withdraw from the Tribunal. This was despite having among other things signed the SADC Treaty and its amendments, as well as the Protocol establishing the Tribunal. The Government had also appointed a judge to the Tribunal, had participated in the Tribunal proceedings